C000177067

HOLBORN VIADUCT TO LEWISHAM

including the Greenwich Park branch

Vic Mitchell and Keith Smith

in association with

Leslie and Philip Davis

Middleton Press

SOUTHERN MP CLASSICS

Cover picture: A view of Holborn Viaduct prior
to 1921 shows ex-LCDR class A1 0-4-4T no. 628
and SECR class D 4-4-0 no. 247. (Lens of Sutton)

Published in the year in which
Holborn Viaduct station closed
and a new City station opened.

First published August 1990

ISBN 0 906520 81 9

© Middleton Press 1990

Design and Laser typesetting -
          Deborah Goodridge
          Barbara Mitchell

Published by Middleton Press
Easebourne Lane
Midhurst, West Sussex
GU29 9AZ
Tel. (0730) 813169

Printed & bound by Biddles Ltd,
Guildford and Kings Lynn

CONTENTS

ACKNOWLEDGEMENTS

In addition to many of those mentioned in the photographic credits, we would like to express our gratitude to R.M.Casserley, Dr.E.Course, G.Croughton, N.Langridge, G.Larkbey, R.Randell, E.Staff, N.Stanyon, and our ever helpful wives.

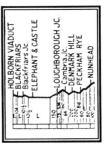

Map to show the former ownership of the railways of South London. Those closed by 1960 are marked with dashes.
(Railway Magazine)

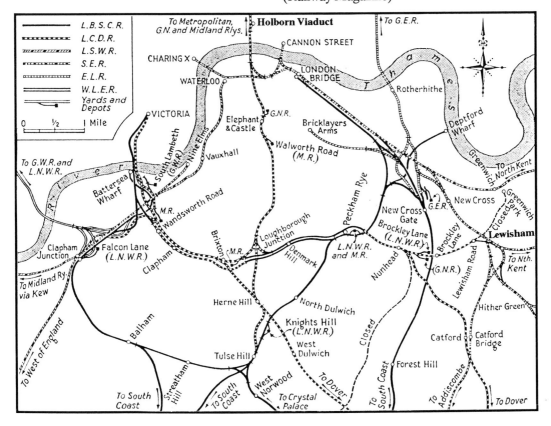

GEOGRAPHICAL SETTING

South to Loughborough Junction, the route was constructed on the Alluvium and River Terrace Gravels of the Lower Thames Valley. Eastwards the line crosses London Clay to Peckham Rye and Woolwich Beds to Nunhead, where it returns onto London Clay again. The Lewisham area and most of the Greenwich Park branch were built on Gravel.

All maps are to the scale of 25" to 1 mile, unless otherwise indicated.

HISTORICAL BACKGROUND

The lines covered by this album were almost entirely built by the London, Chatham and Dover Railway and constitute about half of their London area route mileage. The company's first line to the Metropolis ran from Bromley (South) to Herne Hill, where it divided for the West End and the City.

The line between Herne Hill and Elephant & Castle came into use on 6th October 1862 and the route south to Beckenham followed on 1st July 1863. Extension north to a station on the south bank of the Thames, named Blackfriars, was opened on 1st June 1864. Trains did not cross the river until 21st December 1864, when a temporary terminus at Ludgate Hill (Earl Street) was opened. The permanent station was ready on 1st June 1865 and trains ran through to the Metropolitan Railway at Farringdon Street from 1st January 1866. A spur enabled LCDR trains to run to Moorgate Street from 1st October 1871.

A branch to Crystal Palace (later High Level) was ready for traffic on 1st August 1865 and a branch from this line to Blackheath Hill was opened on 18th September 1871, diverging at Nunhead. This route was extended to Greenwich Park on 1st October 1888 and the Catford Loop, between Nunhead and Shortlands, followed on 1st July 1892.

The area was also served by the London, Brighton & South Coast Railway whose South London Line trains started using the South Bermondsey - East Brixton route on 13th August 1866. Their services between Peckham Rye and Sutton commenced on 1st October 1868. Lewisham had been served by the South Eastern Railway's North Kent trains, from London Bridge, since 30th July 1849.

Later developments in London included an additional bridge over the Thames and a new station at its north end. This was named St. Pauls (now Blackfriars) and was opened on 10th May 1886. The tracks south to Loughborough Junction had been quadrupled in 1866 and an additional terminus added at Holborn Viaduct on 2nd March 1874.

On 1st January 1899, the LCDR from the south ceased to compete with the South Eastern Railway, both being managed by a committee known as the South Eastern & Chatham Railway Managing Committee.

Regular passenger services from the south to Farringdon Street ceased on 30th June 1908 and to Moorgate Street on 1st April 1916.

The other closure affecting the route was the withdrawal of services between Nunhead and Greenwich Park on 1st September 1917. The branch remained dormant until 30th June

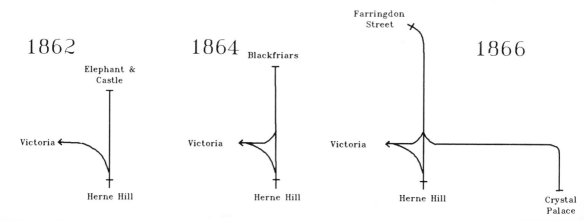

1929, when the southern part was incorporated in the new Nunhead-Lewisham Loop. The remainder was lifted at about that time.

Electrification of passenger services on the route to Nunhead took place on 12th July 1925, two years after the formation of the Southern Railway, and Nunhead to Lewisham followed on 30th September 1935. British Railways was formed in 1948 and closure of the Nunhead - Crystal Palace (High Level) branch followed on 20th September 1954.

Complete closure of the connection to Farringdon took place on 23rd March 1969, after the cessation of through freight services. Fortunately the tunnel was not obstructed and an electrified passenger service between Bedford and Brighton was introduced on 16th May 1988. Holborn Viaduct usage declined and total closure took place on 26th January 1990.

PASSENGER SERVICES

The first service was between Elephant & Castle and Victoria, but this had to operate via Herne Hill initially. From August 1865, the introduction of a service to Crystal Palace provided trains at fairly frequent intervals, north of Elephant & Castle, to Ludgate Hill.

On 3rd August 1866, the LSWR commenced a service from Ludgate Hill to Kingston and to Hounslow, by which time LCDR trains were running to Farringdon Street and GNR stock was operating between Hatfield and Herne Hill.

From 1st January 1869, the LSWR began to run to the City from Wimbledon, via Tulse Hill. In the same year Midland Railway trains began running between Kentish Town and Victoria, via Ludgate Hill. Later, the GNR started a Wood Green-Victoria service. Moorgate Street became the terminus for some LCDR trains from 1871 and long distance ones were terminated at Holborn Viaduct from 1874, when it opened.

From 1878, SER trains used the northern part of the route on a Woolwich-Finsbury Park service, which was later extended to Enfield. These trains were withdrawn in 1907 and all trains to Farringdon ceased in the following year.

Rationalisation of services by the SR meant the transfer of most Kent Coast services, to Charing Cross or Cannon Street in 1925. (Boat trains had been transferred to Victoria on 8th January 1920).

The introduction of local electric services in 1925 and their extension up to 1939, brought a reduction in the number of destinations that could be reached direct from Holborn Viaduct. However, from 1935 it was possible to travel to some of the stations on the Dartford lines, at least in the peak hours.

In recent decades, the basic services have operated to Wimbledon and to Sevenoaks, although Orpington was included for a number of years. May 1988 brought a radical change with the introduction of Thameslink services from various stations from Bedford southwards to stations on the Brighton and Sevenoaks lines. Some trains run via Elephant & Castle while others leave the route at Blackfriars Junction and pass through London Bridge. Guildford was a destination added in 1990 to give the City part of the line its best service ever.

Diagrams to show the evolution of the LCDR lines in the London area.

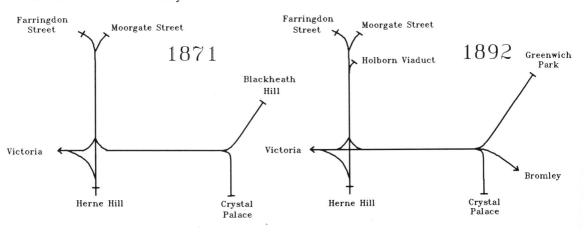

FARRINGDON

The Metropolitan Railway is on the left (upper and lower) of the 1869 survey, the connection to Moorgate starting at West Street Junction (near the word "CHATHAM") and curving underground to a junction under the meat market. This spur was built by the Metropolitan Railway and was closed on 1st April 1916 as a wartime economy measure.

Failure to reopen it resulted in the Metropolitan taking legal action against the Southern Railway for loss of revenue and the lines were subsequently lifted in the late 1920s. Snow Hill station was opened on 1st August 1874, being situated near the words "& DOVER". Near the word "RAILWAY" are

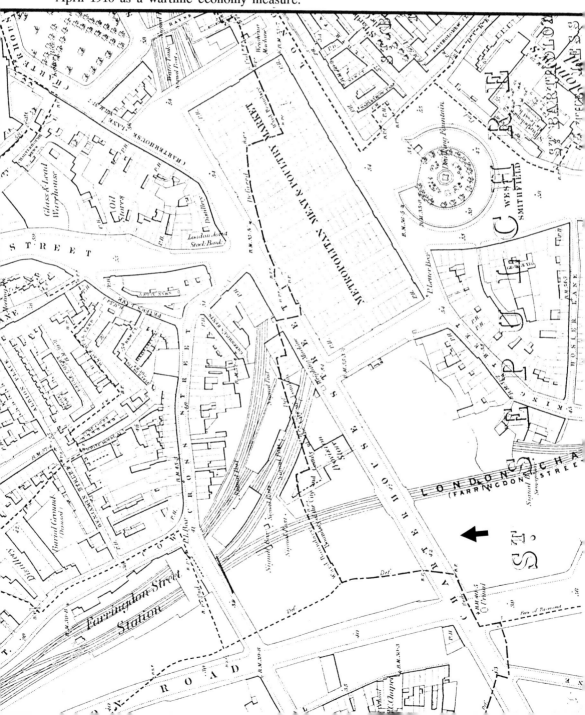

two sidings which were on the site of the future Holborn Viaduct station. The viaduct itself had been completed in 1869 and passed over Farringdon Road which had been constructed over the enclosed Fleet River. The line rises steeply to pass over Ludgate Hill to reach the main LCDR City station of that name, just off the right border. Christ's Hospital is shown, centre top. The school moved to Sussex in 1902 and a station of that name was built nearby, from which a special train ran to London Bridge on 21st September each year (St. Matthew's Day), until 1988. It returned from Holborn Viaduct.

1. An Inner Circle line train stands on the left on 23rd August 1947, while a LNER banking engine stands at Farringdon Junction, where the SR metals commence and diverge to the right. At that time, the wooden platform 4 was served by peak hour trains from Moorgate to LMS and LNER suburban stations. The suffix "Street" was dropped in 1922. (H.C.Casserley)

L. C. & D. R.
SNOW HILL
SNOW HILL   SNOW HILL
TO   (S 5)
KING'S CROSS (MET.)
Change at Aldersgate Street
THIRD   CLASS
1½d.   1½d.
Available on the day of issue only.
See Other Side.
KING'S CROSS (MET.)   KING'S CROSS (MET

028   028

2. A closer look at Farringdon Junction on 27th April 1957, shows class J50 0-6-0T no. 68921 waiting in the banking engine siding, to assist the next down freight train. No. 40028 was one of twenty ex-LMS class 3P 2-6-2Ts to be fitted with condensing equipment for use in the tunnels and is seen taking empty stock to Moorgate for the evening rush hour. (S.C.Nash)

3. Viewed from the brake van of a goods train awaiting assistance, the banking engine approaches the murky atmosphere of the tunnel, having used the crossover seen in the foreground of picture no. 1. The frequency of freight services often meant that it did not have time to enter its siding on the right. (V.Mitchell)

S. E. & C. & D. RYS.
Available Date of issue only (See back.
SNOW HILL   SNOW HILL
TO
BISHOPSGATE.
Change at Moorgate Street
THIRD   CLASS
3d   3d
BISHOPSGATE   BISHOPSGATE

7613   7618

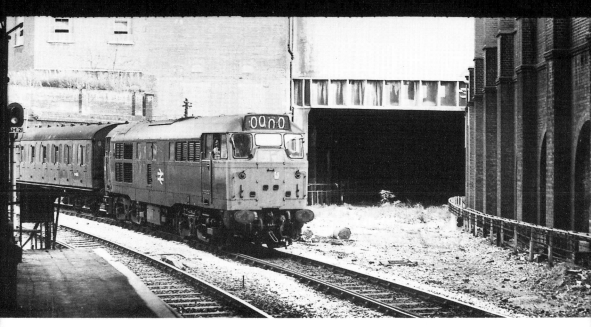

4. After the cessation of cross London freight transfers, the line was closed on 23rd March 1969 and the tunnel remained a monument to the mismanagement of London's transport policy. An Eastern Region suburban service from Moorgate passes by on 19th August 1976. (E.Wilmshurst)

5. The Moorgate line was electrified (overhead 25,000 volts) for use by London Midland trains, Eastern Region trains having been diverted through the former Northern City tunnels. Farringdon Junction was reinstated, fitted with conductor rails, and opened for the new Thameslink services on 16th May 1988. The dual voltage class 319 units change to overhead collection in Farringdon station, this example being no. 319054, en route from Purley to Luton on 12th February 1990. (J.Scrace)

6. Opened eight years after the line came into use, the station first handled passengers on the 1st August 1874. The gloomy location is reputed to have necessitated whitewashing weekly. The up platform is seen on 4th April 1933, as empty stock is signalled into one of the four subterranean berthing sidings.
(O.J.Morris / Lens of Sutton)

L. C. & D. R.
SNOW HILL
TO
KING'S CROSS G.N.
THIRD CLASS
Fare 1½d.
Available on the day of issue only.
See Other Side.
KING'S CROSS G N   KING'S CROSS G. N.

9075   9075

7. LNER class N1 0-6-2T no. 4565 adds to the soot encrustations as it runs south on the same day. The entrance to the sidings and the profile of the signal box are on the left. The platforms had last seen passengers on 1st June 1916. (O.J.Morris / Lens of Sutton)

Met'n. & L. C. & D. Rv's.
MOORGATE STREET
TO (S. 6)
SNOW HILL.
SECOND CLASS
2d. 2d.
Available on the day of issue only
See Other Side.
SNOW HILL. SNOW HILL.
8215 8215

8. Holborn Viaduct (Low Level) was the more helpful name applied after 1st May 1912 and the nameboard on the up platform was still visible when photographed in July 1948. There were entrances to the station from the High Level station, from Holborn Viaduct itself and from Snow Hill. (J.J.Smith)

9. Snow Hill signal box was located under the road of that name and was brightly polished internally but soot coated outside, never being washed by rain. Although bounded by colour light signals, it controlled much mechanical equipment and is seen in 1953. (P.Hay)

10. A northward view from near the signal box on 11th July 1954, shows ex LNER 0-6-2T no. 69435 waiting for a banker to help raise the 9.30am Hitchin to Brighton excursion up to Ludgate. Another excursion that used this route is illustrated in picture no. 101 in our *Charing Cross to Dartford* album. The wall on the right marks the alignment of the former curve towards Moorgate. (J.J.Smith)

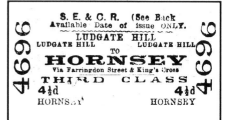

11. The 5.0pm parcels from Kings Cross to Victoria was hauled by class J50 0-6-0T no. 68917 on 9th September 1956. The down platform (right) was cut back when the catch points in the foreground were installed. Two of the berthing sidings were reinstated in 1990. (J.J.Smith)

HOLBORN VIADUCT

12. The terminus was opened on 2nd March 1874, to reduce congestion at Ludgate Hill, and is seen in 1913. It was for use by Kent Coast trains which split into City and West End portions at Herne Hill, hence only short platforms were required. A similar practice had already been established by the LBSCR at East Croydon. (P.Rutherford)

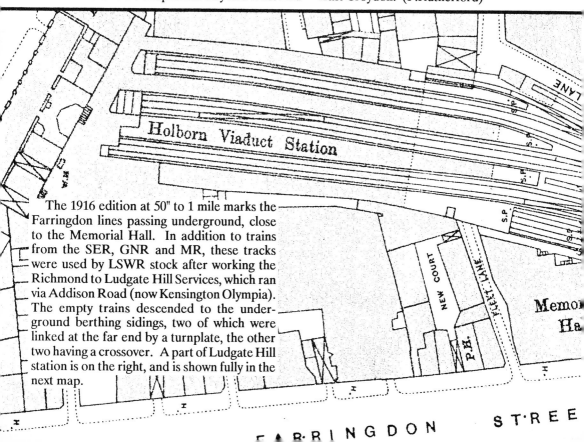

Holborn Viaduct Station

The 1916 edition at 50" to 1 mile marks the Farringdon lines passing underground, close to the Memorial Hall. In addition to trains from the SER, GNR and MR, these tracks were used by LSWR stock after working the Richmond to Ludgate Hill Services, which ran via Addison Road (now Kensington Olympia). The empty trains descended to the underground berthing sidings, two of which were linked at the far end by a turnplate, the other two having a crossover. A part of Ludgate Hill station is on the right, and is shown fully in the next map.

NEW COURT

FLEET LANE

LANE

P.H.

Memo
Ha

FARRINGDON STREE

13. Viewed from the narrow platform 6 in about 1921, class D 4-4-0 no. 247 blows off alongside ex-LCDR 0-4-4T no. 628, a type commonly used on suburban services. The railings on the left are above the incline to Farringdon. (Lens of Sutton)

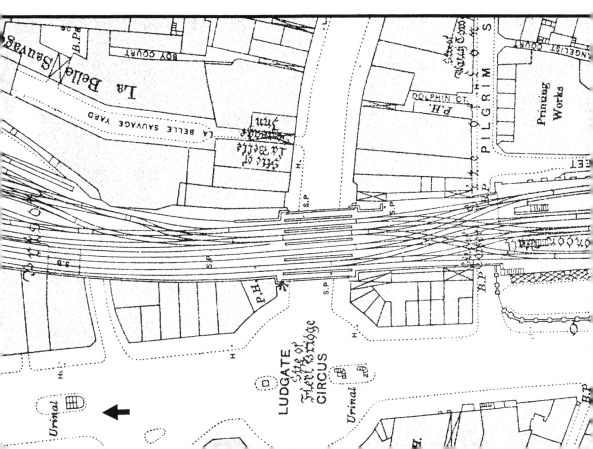

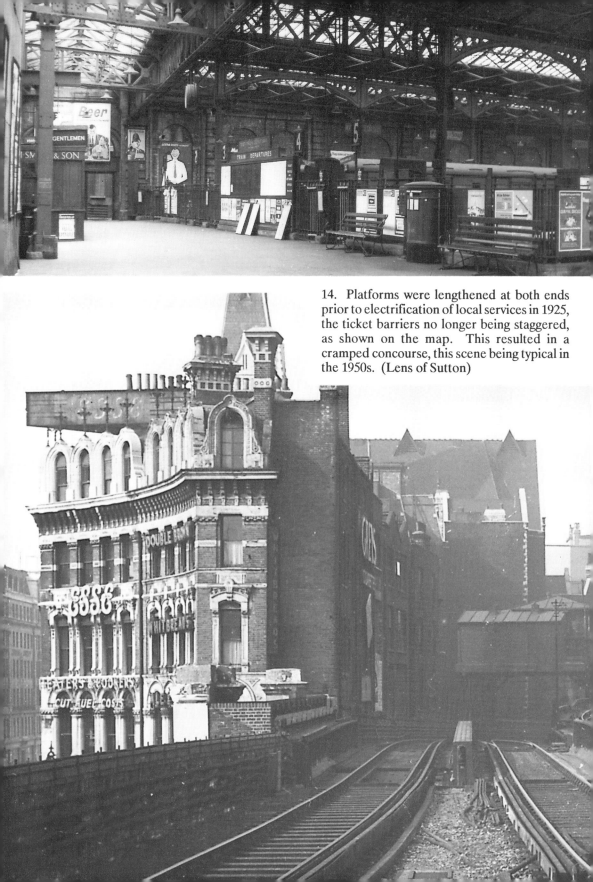

14. Platforms were lengthened at both ends prior to electrification of local services in 1925, the ticket barriers no longer being staggered, as shown on the map. This resulted in a cramped concourse, this scene being typical in the 1950s. (Lens of Sutton)

15.   After the bombing of WWII, little remained of the six-storey LCDR hotel, which
had opened in November 1877.   The station
had been popular with travellers to Europe
from areas north of London, as the cross
London journey was minimal.
(Lens of Sutton)

16. A northward view in 1950 shows the Farringdon lines descending under the signal box,
the crossover for returning banking engines
being visible beyond the girders of Ludgate
Hill bridge.   The approach to the terminus is
on the right.   (J.H.Aston)

17. The signal box was fitted with 86 levers to control the area electrically from 21st March 1926 until 10th March 1974. Thereafter, operation was from a panel in Blackfriars box. Remains of Ludgate Hill station are evident in the distance in April 1955. (D.Cullum)

York Road (G.N.) ....dep	1021				1057			118	c		138		1155		1210	c		1247			1248	c					1 31		1 53			2 8
King's Cross (Met.) ,,	1023		1038	1047	11 1		1121		1124	1141		1154		1212	1215	1218	1224	1238	1246		1 3	3 1	20		1 28	1 38		1 57	2 1		2 25
Moorgate Street ,,	1024		1038	1046	1058		1118		1124	1135		1155		1212	1215	1218	1224	1238	1246		1 3	3 1	20		1 23	1 38		1 53	2 3		2 25
Aldersgate Street ,,	1026		1040	1048	11 0		112c		1126	1140		157		1214	1217	1220	1226	1240	1248		1 5	3 1	22		1 26	1 40		1 55	2 5		2 25
Farringdon Street ,,	1031		1043	1051	11 7		1125		1135	1146		12 3		1218	1221	1225	1232	1245	1255		1 10	17	27		1 34	1 46		2 1	2 9		2 29
Ludgate Hill	1040		1050	1058	1113	118	1129	1135	1140	1153		12 8	1220	1224	1226	1230	1237	1242	1250	0 1	5 1	15	25	31	35	40	53	2	5 2	17	24 2 35
Blackfriars Bridge	1042		1052	11 0	1115	1120	1131	1137	1142	1155		1210	1222	1225	1228	1232	1239	1344	1252	2 1	7 1	17	27	33	37	42	55		2 7	19	26 2 37
Borough Road	1045		1055	11 3	1118	1123	1134	1140	1145	1158		1213	1225	1228	1231		1242	1247	1255	5		20	30		1 40		1 58		2 10	22	2 40
Elephant and Castle	1047		1057	11 5	1120	1125	1136	1142	1147	12 0		1215	1227	1230	1234	1244	1249	1257	7 1	11	22	32	37	42	46 2	0		2 12	24	2 39 2 42
Walworth Road	1050		11 0	11 8	1123	1128	1139	1145	1150	12 3		1218	1230	1234	1237	1239	1247	1252	0 1	10 1	14	25	35	40	43	49 2	3		2 15	27	2 33 2 45
Camberwell New Road	1053		11 3	1111	1126	1131	1142	1148	1153	12 6		1221	1233	1236	1240	1242	1250	1255 1	3 1	13 1	17	28	38	43	48	52 2	6		2 18	30	2 36 2 48
Loughborough Road	1056		11 6	1114	1129	1134	1145		1156	12 9		1224	1236	1239		1245	1253	1258	6 1	16		31	41	45 1	51	55 2	9		2 21	33	2 39 2 51
Brixton & South Stckwell	1059		11 3	11 9	1117	1132	1137	1148		1159	1212	1218	1227	1239	1242		1245	1256 1	1 1	9 1	19		34 1	44		1 54	58 2	12 2	16 2	24 2	36 2 42 2 54
Clapham & NorthStckwll	11 2		11 6	1112	1129	1135	1140	1151		12 2	1215	1221	1230	1242	1245		1251	1255 1	4 1	12 1	22		37 1	47 b	d 1	57 2	1 2	15 2	19 2	27 2 39 2 45 2 57
Wandsworth Road	11 4	11 8	11 9	1114	1122	1137	1142	1153		12 4	1217	1223	1232	1244	1247		1253 1	1	6 1	14 1	24		39 1	49		1 59	2	3 2	17 2	21 2	29 2 41 2 47 2 59
Clapham Junc. 40,42	11 9					1922												a							2 22				a		3 3
Kensington ......arr	1125			b		1157			a				1 0		a					a					2 15				a		3 3
Battersea Park(Yrk.Rd.)	e		1117	1125	1140		1156		12 7				1235				1256	1	4 1	9 1	17 1	27		1 42	52			2		2 32 2 44	3 2
Grosvenor Road		1112	1119	1127	1142		1158		12 9				1227	1237		1251			1 5 1	6 1	12 1	19 1	29		1 44	54			2	8	2 25 3 42 46	3 4
Victoria ......arr		1117	1124	1132	1147 S W	12 3 S W	1214		1232	1242 S W	1256		3 1	111	171	241	34 8 W	1 49	1 59		3 W 2	13		2	30 2	39 2	51 S W 3	9

a Run through between Victoria and King's Cross (G.N.); change at Farringdon St. by all other Trains. b Through Trains to Kentish Town and Finchley Road on Midland Line. c Run to and from the Main Line Platforms.

Walworth Rd., Ele'phCastle, Borough Rd., & Blackfriars. d Run to and from the Siding Platform, Loughborough Road. e Change at Clapham Jn. kman's Train, 3rd cl. *,* Passengers to and from Stations on the Metropolitan Line change at Farringdon Street. ¶ Change at Farringdon Street.

Part of the midday down service on weekdays in June 1869.

18. A panorama from the signal box on 7th September 1958 includes class D1 no. 31741 taking water at platform 2, having worked the 10.35am parcels train from Ramsgate. Owing to the site being tapered, platforms 2 and 3 could not be lengthened and therefore devoid of conductor rails, being largely used for parcels and newspapers. This picture also shows that the terminus was partially built above the Farringdon lines to gain space. (J.J.Smith)

19. The bomb damaged station was completely rebuilt and is seen in September 1963, soon after completion. From 15th June 1964, the station was closed from 2pm Saturdays until midnight on Sundays. (British Rail)

20. Above the station, nine floors for commericial office purposes were provided and are shown in 1974. The entire structure was listed for demolition, following complete closure of the station on 26th January 1990. (British Rail)

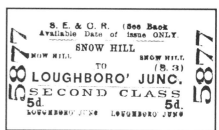

S. E. & C. R. (See Back)
Available Date of Issue ONLY.
SNOW HILL

SNOW HILL   SNOW HILL
          TO   (8. 3)
LOUGHBORO' JUNC.
SECOND CLASS
5d.   5d.
LOUGHBORO' JUNC   LOUGHBORO' JUNC
5877   5877

Extract from Bradshaw for July 1880, showing
the weekday early morning arrivals.

Victoria ......dep								
Grosvenor Road...								
Battersea P. (Y.R.)								
Clapham Junc. d								
Wandsworth Road.								
Clapham & N. Stkwll								
Brixton & S. Stckwll								
Loughborough Junc								
Camberwell New Rd								
Walworth Road....								
Elephant and Castle								
Borough Road								
Blackfriars Bridge.								
Ludgate Hill								
Holborn Viaduct a								
Snow Hill [208 ..								
Aldersgate St 156..								
Moorgate Street..								
Farringdon St.								
King's Cross {Met. {G.N.								
Kentish Town ..,,								

21. The short platforms (2 & 3) were removed in 1973, no. 6 ceased to be used in 1974, leaving the three platforms photographed in April 1987. Since June 1981, the station had closed at 19.30 and, from 16th May 1988, no trains moved between 09.18 and 15.28. The platform canopy dates from 1967. (A.C.Mott)

22. A Thameslink service climbs the 1 in 39 gradient from Farringdon on 18th January 1990, while empty stock stands at platform 3 and demolition contractors begin removal of the viaduct. Thameslink services were suspended between 13th and 28th May 1990 to allow the removal of the bridge over Ludgate Hill and the lowering of the tracks between Snow Hill and Blackfriars. (A.C.Mott)

ST. PAULS THAMESLINK

23. Prior to the removal of Ludgate Hill bridge, work commenced on the construction of the new station, behind the white boards. It necessitated raising the road level two metres and so work was restricted until the bridge was removed on 13th May 1990. One station entrance would be provided initially, near the bus, and one on Holborn Viaduct would follow in 1991. (A.C.Mott)

24. The Bovis board is on the site of the former Holborn Viaduct station concourse. A Brighton bound class 319 unit runs onto the freshly aligned track as it approaches the City's newest station, opened on 29th May 1990 and photographed two days later. (V.Mitchell)

25. Viewed from platform 5 at Blackfriars on the same day, it is clear that the new station is built within a concrete box. The 1974 bridge in the foreground was lowered at its far end by 1.26m (4ft) to reduce the gradient, which is an amazing 1 in 29. A scissors crossover at the bottom of the incline is for use by terminating trains. (V.Mitchell)

LUDGATE HILL

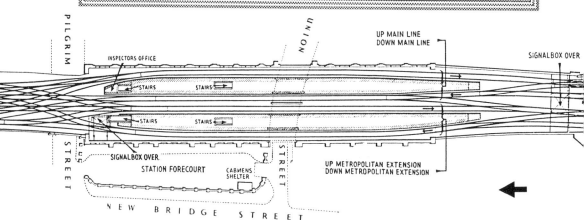

A plan from the 1890s reveals two narrow platforms, which often became dangerously overcrowded. The tracks were spanned by a wooden framed roof, with timber supports. (Railway Magazine)

Concentration of long distance traffic at Holborn Viaduct meant that one island platform could be dispensed with, thus allowing widening of the other for use by Moorgate trains. The work took place in 1910-12. (Railway Magazine)

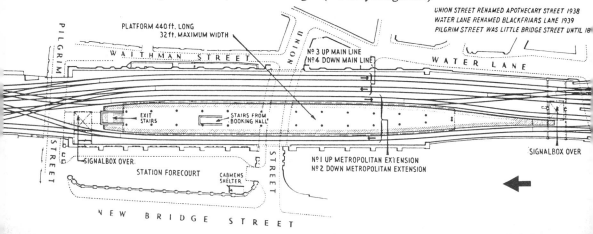

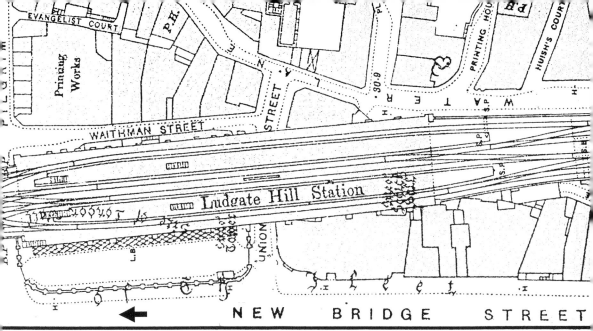

EVANGELIST COURT

P.H.

PILGRIM

Printing Works

WAITHMAN STREET

STREET

Ludgate Hill Station

L.B.

UNION

W A T E R

·30·9

PRINTING HOU

HUISH'S COURT

NEW   BRIDGE   STREET

This 1895 map at 50" to 1 mile is continuous with the one for Holborn Viaduct, the hatched area representing the glazed canopy in the station forecourt. Passenger services ceased on 3rd March 1929, the platforms being of insufficient length for electric trains.

upper left

This impressive station was opened to serve the City of London on 1st June 1865, 21 years before the present Blackfriars station came into use. Sadly, it was soon obscured by a row of indifferent shops, became eclipsed by adjacent stations and fell into a steady decline.

26. A southward view after WWII reveals that, ironically, the redundant station suffered little during the hostilities. The ornate brickwork once carried a roof over the four tracks and associated platforms. (Lens of Sutton)

27. A northward view from Blackfriars, in about 1950, shows empty stock from Stewarts Lane to Cannon Street approaching the original bridge over the Thames. The train had reversed at Ludgate Hill station, which was demolished in 1974 by which time only the two tracks on the right were in use. An electrified siding was laid in the vacated space. (J.J.Smith)

Weekday afternoon departures in July 1906.

Week days—																								
Midland Station.	c	aft	a	aft	aft	c	aft	aft	aft	a	c	b	aft	aft	aft	b	a	aft	aft	a	aft	aft		
Kentish Town ...dep	...1 37			1s51	2	1			2s56	3 8	3 19	3 22		3 54	4 21		4 31	4e15	4 58	...	5e15			
York Rd. (G.N.). n	....	1s39	1 52		1 59	...	2 24		2 44	3 9	...	3 33		3 53	4 14	...	4 33	4 39	4 52	5 8	5 12	5 22		
King's C. (Met.). n	....	1 45	1 55		2	2 22	8	2 27	2 47	3 12	3 15	3 26	3 26	3 56	4 17	4 28	4 36	4 42	4 55	5 11	5 15	5 25		
Farringdon St... n	....	1 49	1 59		2	2 2	2 31	...	2 51	3 16	3 19	3 30	3 40	...	4 0	4 21	4 32	4 40	4 46	4 59	5 15	5 19	5 29	
Moorgate St. .... n	....	1 41	51		...2	3 2	22	...	2 33	2 47	3 1	...3	3 25	...	3 49	5 4	25	...	4 53	5	4	...	5 25	5 37
Aldersgate St... n	1 43	1 53	...		2 15	2 24	...	2 35	2 49	3	3	...3	27	...	3 51	4	7	4 27	...	4 55	5	6	5 27	5 39
Snow Hill.... n	1 46	1 56	2	2	2 17	2 26	2 33	2 37	2 53	7	3 19	3 29	3 34	3 42	3 52	4	9	4 30	4 34	4 43	4 57	5	8	5 17
Holborn Viaduct																								
Ludgate Hill	1 53	2	0	2	7	2 16	2 21	2 23	2 36	2 40	2 57	3 12	3 23	3 33	3 39	3 45	3 56	4 15	4 34	4 38	4 47	5	1 5	11 5 20 5 34 5 46
St. Paul's																								
Borough Road	...2	4	2	19	...2	26	...	3	1 3	16	3 26	...3	43	3 59	4 19	...	4 43	4 52	5	6	...	5 28	5 58
Elephant & Castle...	1 57	2	6	2 14	2 21	2 28	2 36		2 44	3	3 18	3 28	3 38	3 45		4	14	4 45	4 55	5	8	...	5 27 5 40 5 50
Walworth Road	...2	9	2 17	2 24	2 31	...	2 47	3	6	3 21	3 31	...	3 48		4	4	24	...	4 48	4 58	5 11	...	5 30 5 43 5 53
Camberwell New Rd	...2	12	2 20	2 27	2 34	...	2 50	3	9	3 24	3 34	...3	51	4	7	4 27	...	4 51	5	1 5	14	...	5 33 5 46 5 56
Loughboro' Junc. ..	2	3 2	14	2 23	2 30	2 37	2 42	...	2 53	3 11	3 26	3 37	3 44	3 54		4	9	4 30	4 43	4 54	5	4 5	17 5 22 5 36 5 40 5 58
Brixton & S.S.....	...2	17	2 25		2 40	...		2 56	3 14	3 29	3 40	...	3 57		4	12	4 33	4 47	4 57	5	7 5	20 5 25 5 39 5 52 6	1
Clapham & N.S.....	...2	20	2 31		2 43	...		2 59	3 17	3 32	3 43	...	4	0		4	15	4 36	4 50	5	0 5	10 5 23 5 28 5 42 5 55 6	4
Wandsworth Road...	...2	22	2 34		2 45	...		3	1 3	19	3 34	3 45	...	4	2		4	17	4 38	4 52	5	2 5	12 5 25 5 30 5 44 5 57 6	6
Clapham Jn.* arr.	...2	27					3	6	...3	41									5 30		...6	2		
Battersea Park Rd...	...2	37		2	48	...	3	22	...3	48	...4	5		4	20	4 41	4 54	5	5 15	...	5 33 5 47	...6	9
Grosvenor Road....	...2	39		2	50	...	3	26	...3	50	...4	7		4	22	4 43	4 56	5	7 5	17	...	5 35 5 49	...6	11
Victoria ...... arr.	...2	44		2	53	...	3	55	...4	12	4	48	5	1 5	12 5	29	...	5 40 5 54	...6	16		

a Run through from King's Cross (G.N.) to Victoria; change at Aldersgate Street by other Trains. b Through Trains from Kentish Town on Midland Line. c Run to the Crystal Palace Line Platforms at Loughboro' Junction, and the Main Line Platforms at Borough Road, Elephant and Castle, Walworth Road, and Camberwell New Road. e Except Saturdays. g Except Mondays; starts from Snow Hill on Mondays. h Midland Trains, 1 & 3 class. s Saturdays only.
* Mid Battersea, 1¼ miles to Clapham.

BLACKFRIARS

28. The station was opened on 10th May 1886, as a further move towards reducing congestion at Ludgate Hill. Two through platforms were provided (left), the remaining ones being for termination. This is a northward view in 1913. (P.Rutherford)

29. Photographed in the mid-1920s, the two central tracks still had platforms on both sides. The arrangement of the terminal platforms was altered in readiness for the introduction of electric traction in June 1925. (Lens of Sutton)

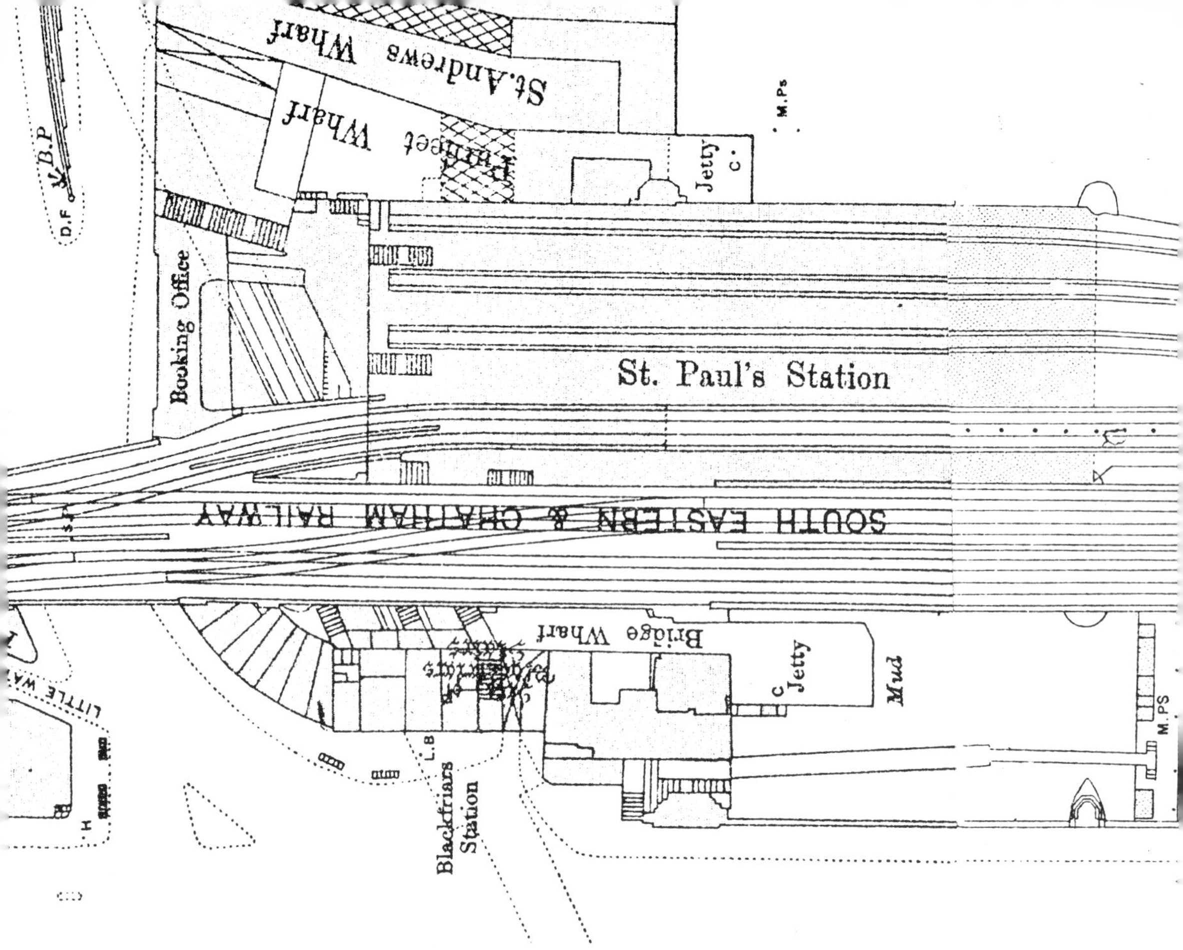
St.Andrews Wharf
Puddle Dock (crossed out); Wharf
Jetty
M.Ps
Booking Office
St. Paul's Station
SOUTH EASTERN & CHATHAM RAILWAY
Bridge Wharf
Jetty
Mud
M.PS
L.B
Blackfriars Station
LITTLE

30. A Gillingham service departs from platform 4 on 1st July 1939, the last day of regular steam working of passenger services on the line. However, a few nocturnal newspaper trains also carried passengers but otherwise Holborn Viaduct became the first SR terminus to have all electric passenger services. (H.C.Casserley)

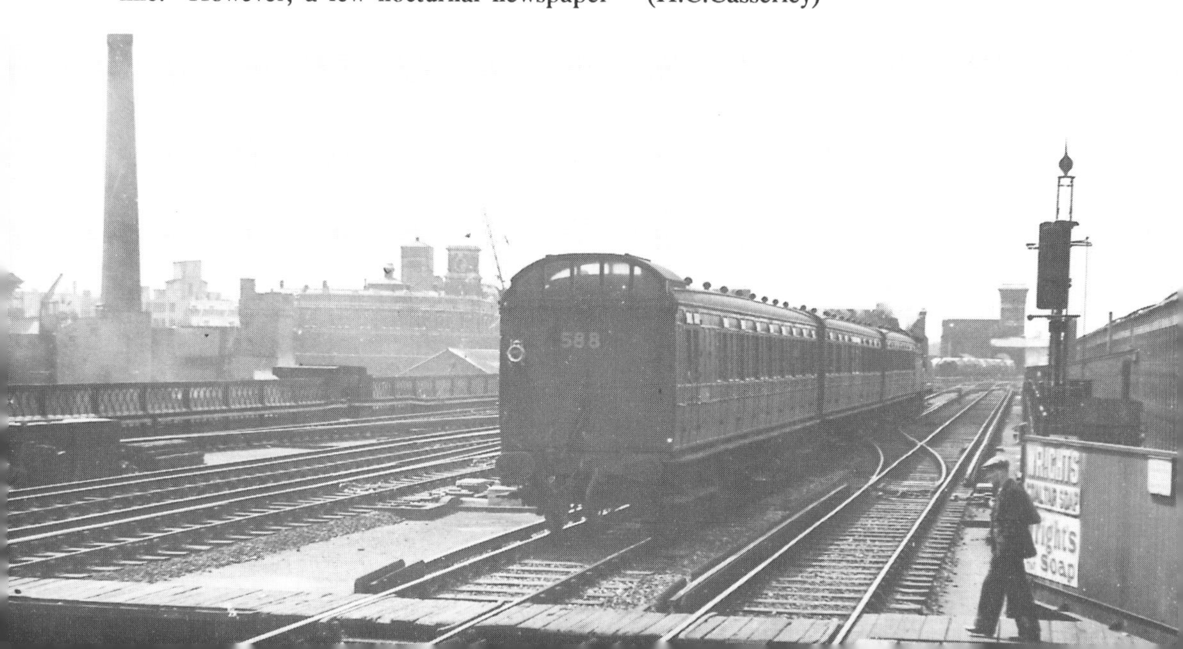
588
Soap

The 1916 map at 50" to 1 mile is almost continuous with that for Ludgate Hill and shows seven platforms under the roof and four through tracks to the west. The station was named St. Paul's until 1st February 1937, when an Underground station on the Central line was renamed from "Post Office" to "St. Pauls".

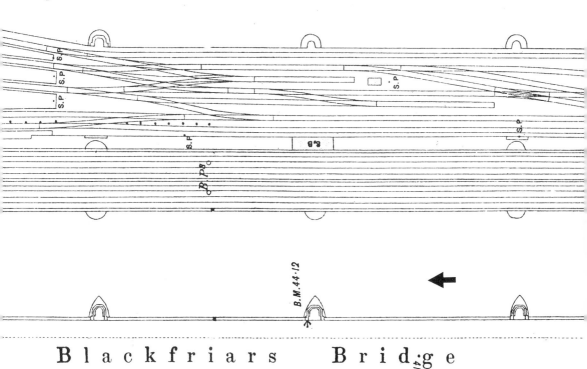

B l a c k f r i a r s   B r i d g e

31. Carved into the stone columns were names of possible destinations of former travellers, these ranging from Gravesend to Darmstadt and Herne Bay to Florence. During the re-building in 1973-77, the stones were cleaned and incorporated in the new booking hall. (Lens of Sutton)

32. The interior was drab and grimy, the knots rising from the well worn floorboards. The up platform for Holborn Viaduct was by the wall in the background. By the early 1980s over 16,000 people were using the station on every business day. (Lens of Sutton)

upper right

33. Compare this picture with no. 29 to see how the platforms were altered and extended. Ex-LSWR class T9 4-4-0 waits to leave with a ramblers' excursion to Tring on 10th October 1954, while an up train crosses the original bridge on the left. (S.C.Nash)

→

34. A 1955 photograph includes the bridge over Queen Victoria Street, Ludgate Hill station and Holborn Viaduct signal box. The platforms were boarded to reduce their weight, as they were built over the river. (J.J.Smith)

35. The roof was of slender proportions, again to reduce weight. The London Underground Circle Line and the Blackfriars Underpass also run under the station, which is adjacent to the Mermaid Theatre and Puddle Dock. (Lens of Sutton)

36. The rebuilt station was formally reopened by the Lord Mayor of London on 30th November 1977, but much of the southern part of the roof steelwork was retained. Sadly the new cladding bears no relation to the arch profile. A Cricklewood to Orpington service calls on 24th May 1989, the Thameslink trains providing a great increase in traffic at the station which was still devoid of a buffet in 1990. (A.C.Mott)

37. The construction of the first railway bridge was delayed until the design of the road bridge had been finalised, as it was essential that the piers were in line. The 1864 bridge was of lattice design with arched bracings. (D.Cullum coll.)

38. The lattice structure was corroded beyond repair, was also redundant and therefore was dismantled in 1984-85. This 1990 view reveals the 1886 bridge and the piers that were constructed in the 1860s. (J.Scrace)

39. The LCDR crests on the southern abut-
ments were retained and renovated, making a
highly colourful feature on the South Bank.

The stonework came from the Westminster
Bridge that was demolished in 1861.
(J.Scrace)

BLACKFRIARS GOODS

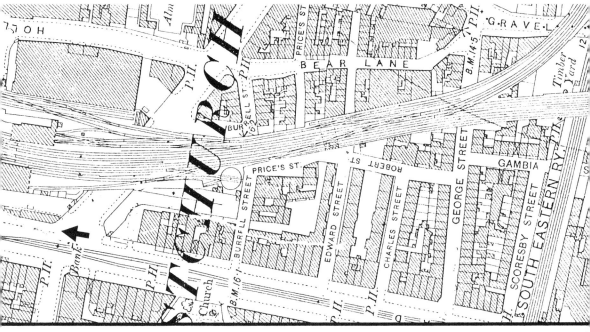

The 1894 survey shows (left) the passenger station that was in use at the south end of Blackfriars Bridge between 1st June 1864 and 30th October 1885, when it was closed following the opening of St. Pauls. Lower right is the SER's line to Charing Cross and upper right is the 1878 spur which allowed that company's trains to reach the GNR via London Bridge and Farringdon. Lower left is the terminus of the horse-worked tramway, opened in 1871 along Blackfriars Road, and above it is the first Blackfriars station. From 1885 until 1964, it was used as part of the goods depot.

The LCDR's first terminus is seen on the south bank of the Thames. Although used by passengers for under twenty years, most of the structure remained standing until 1968. The lattice girder bridge was taken out of traffic on 27th June 1969. (Railway Magazine)

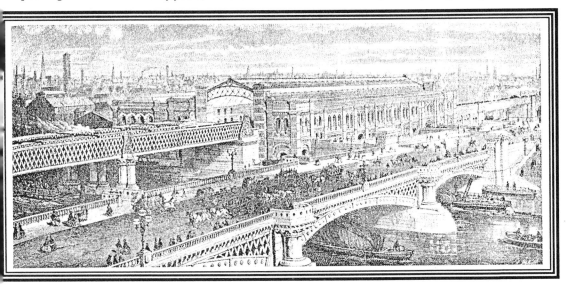

40. A southward view from the new bridge in
April 1955 shows the original Blackfriars
Station at the end of the older bridge, on the
right. The other brick buildings (centre and

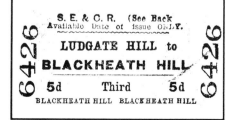

left) accommodated hoists which transferred
wagons to and from the wharf lines.
(British Rail)

41. Viewed from the former passenger platform on a misty February day in 1957, a class J50 0-6-0T plods across the bridge with a transfer freight from Ferme Park, north of Finsbury Park on the Eastern Region. On the right is the companion to the crest seen in picture no. 39. Carriage berthing sidings now occupy the site. (P.Hay)

42. On the left, the two "Market Sidings" enter the former passenger station at the south end. The remainder of the goods depot is shown on the right, along with two buildings for wagon hoists, two hoists being housed in that behind the engine and one in the other. Class J50 no. 68982 is calling to detach vans from the 5.0pm parcels service from Kings Cross to Victoria on 7th June 1959. (J.J.Smith)

43. Further south, ex-LMS 0-6-0T no. 47211 reaches Blackfriars Junction, with freight from the Midland Region on 20th December 1958. The signal box is beyond the brake van and a class D1 4-4-0 stands in the Market Sidings in the distance. (J.J.Smith)

44. The 119-miniature lever junction box was situated off the left margin of picture no. 42 and was in use from 11th August 1946 until 14th February 1982. It replaced a temporary box made necessary by the destruction of the 1926 one by enemy action on 17th April 1941. The bridge over Southwark Street was completely wrecked at the same time. (J.Scrace)

BOROUGH ROAD

45. The 1894 edition shows that the station had platforms on all four tracks. It was opened with the line on 1st June 1864, when the railway had no effective competition. The tramways marked were electrified in 1904 and siphoned off most local passenger traffic, causing the station to be closed on 1st April 1907. Ironically, the tramways depot is adjacent to the station. The Hill Street crossovers are near the top of the map. The signal box of that name spans the tracks and closed on 21st March 1926.

ELEPHANT & CASTLE

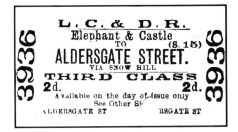

46. A 1958 southward view shows the connection to the GNR coal depot sidings on the New Kent Road bridge. The depot is marked on the next map. Traffic commenced in 1871 and soon five trains were operated to the depot each day. Coal was discharged by gravity into hoppers until closure on 1st July 1963. (British Rail)

47. Looking north in 1913, we see the main lines on the right and the "Metropolitan Extension" lines on the left. The LSWR trains used the latter after the quadrupling had been completed in 1866, as a result of that company having lent the impoverished LCDR substantial sums to complete the line. (P.Rutherford)

The 1895 map has the station in the centre of the left page, with the GNR's coal depot to the left of it. A traverser enabled wagons to be moved into the different sidings. In the centre of the right page is the MR's Walworth coal depot, which required turntables as well as a traverser for its operation.

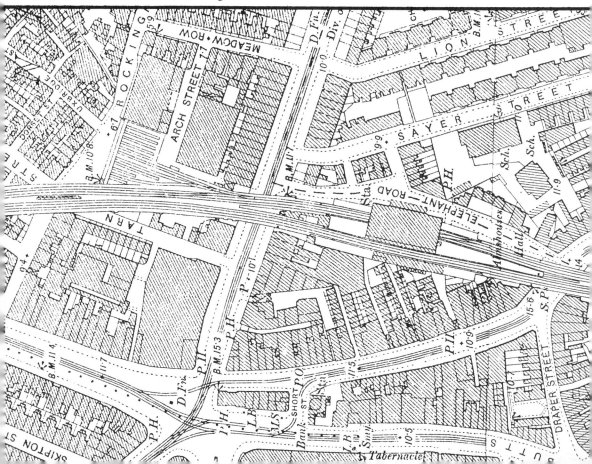

48. The 1.08pm Holborn Viaduct to Gillingham service was headed by class D1 no. 1747 on 1st July 1939. The signal box was destroyed early in WWII and replaced by a new one on 2nd June 1941. (H.C.Casserley)

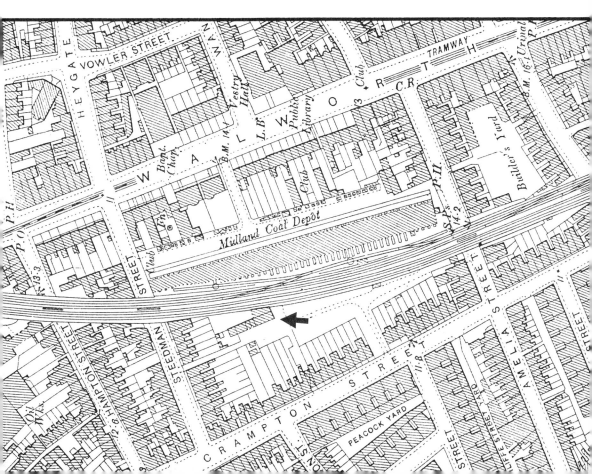

49. The station had received SR style lights and nameboards sometime before this down freight from the LMS passed through on 20th October 1939. Destinations included Feltham, Battersea, Herne Hill, Brockley Lane and Hither Green. (Lens of Sutton)

L. C. & D. R.
Elephant & Castle
TO (S.99)
SNOW HILL.
THIRD CLASS
1½d. 1½d
Available on the 'ay of issue only.
See Side.
SNOW HILL SNOW HILL
8130 8130

51. Extensive bomb damage on 11th May 1941 necessitated the provision of new canopies after WWII. This is the view towards Black-friars in 1952, the year in which London trams ceased to operate. (D.Cullum)

50. Photographed on the same day, class N1 0-6-2T no.4599 runs through platform 1, en route to Ferme Park, where all northbound LNER freights terminated. About 70% of trains passing through Snow Hill Tunnel also ran through Elephant & Castle, the others travelling via London Bridge. (J.R.W.Kirkby coll.)

S. E. & C. & L. YS.
ELEPHANT & CASTLE
ELEPHANT & C ELEPHANT & C
TO (S.14)
STREATHAM
Via Herne Hill & Tulse Hill
THIRD CLASS
5d 5d
Available on the day of issue only
See Other Side
STREATHAM STREATHAM
5162 5162

52. The Elephant Road entrance, on the east side, had been subject to bomb scarring and alterations. Note the unusual platform support on the pavement. (Lens of Sutton)

L. C. & D. R.
DOG TICKET.
Accompanied by Passenger.
LUDGATE HILL
TO
VICTORIA,
GREENWICH, CRYSTAL PALACE,
SHORTLANDS
or Intermediate Station.
For Conditions of Conveyance see back
Rate   3d.
5550   5550

53. Bomb sites were a feature of London life for nearly twenty years after WWII. This one faced passengers emerging from the station into Elephant Road for many years. (Lens of Sutton)

54. Class 700 no.30687 takes the down local line with a RCTS railtour, while a member of staff picks up the whitewash bucket, having finished whitening the platform edge. The tour was of London freight lines and took place on 5th October 1957. (D.Cullum coll.)

S. E. & C. & D. RYS.
Available Date of issue only (See back
ELEPHANT & CASTLE
ELEPHANT & J.   ELEPHANT & J.
TO   (S.58)
CAMBERWELL NEW ROAD
THIRD   CLASS
1½d.   1½d.
CAMBERWELL N. R   CAMBERWELL N. R
1757   1757

55. In recent years, only the island platform has been in use outside the peak hours. The 13.41 Cricklewood to Sevenoaks stands at platform 2 on 16th February 1990, up trains running, unconventionally, on the right. (J.Scrace)

56. Class 319 units on the Luton-Purley service pass on 22nd February 1990, as the London skyline continues its endless evolution. While the east side has been cleaned, the other entrance has been dramatically transformed. Now it is situated in a new enclosed shopping centre. (J.Scrace)

WALWORTH COAL SIDINGS

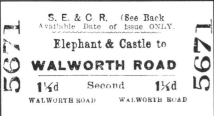

S. E. & C. R. (See Back
Available Date of issue ONLY.

Elephant & Castle to

WALWORTH ROAD

1½d   Second   1½d

WALWORTH ROAD   WALWORTH ROAD

5671   5671

57. As shown on the last map, the sidings were on the east side of the line. Established by the Midland Railway in 1871, the 30 sidings could each take two or three wagons, largely under cover. Ex-LMS 0-6-0T no.47203 waits in the siding on 25th September 1956, as ex-LNER 0-6-0T no.68917 runs south, bound for Hither Green. (J.J.Smith)

58. Photographed on 1st March 1957, Walworth Coal Sidings box towers into the mist while the local shunting horse rests near the turntable. The large pipe on the 3F was for diverting exhaust steam to the water tanks to condense it while working underground. (J.J.Smith)

59. Seen on the same day, the box closed on 15th February 1970. The coal sidings were modernised in 1957-58 and were subsequently discharging about 70,000 tons of fuel per annum. The roof was removed and power capstans fitted but the depot closed on 30th April 1973. (R.C.Riley)

2nd-SINGLE SINGLE-2nd

3011

Elephant & Castle   to
Elephant&Castle   Elephant&Castle
St.MaryCray   St.Mary Cray
ST. MARY CRAY
Via Herne Hill or Ravensbourne
(S)   2/3   FARE   2/3   (B)
For conditions see over For conditions see over

3011

60. A view from the signal box on 1st March 1957 shows the connections to the sidings and ex-LMS 3P 2-6-2T no.40028 southbound with milk tankers. The leading one is demountable - note the road wheels. (R.C.Riley)

61. At Newington Vestry Depot, domestic refuse was loaded into railway wagons, this traffic often giving rise to complaints about smell on its journey to Longfield Sidings, between Meopham and Fawkham. Goods inward probably included the visible building materials. (A.Riley coll.)

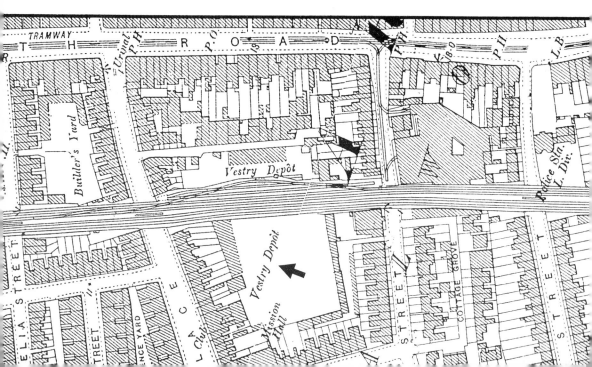

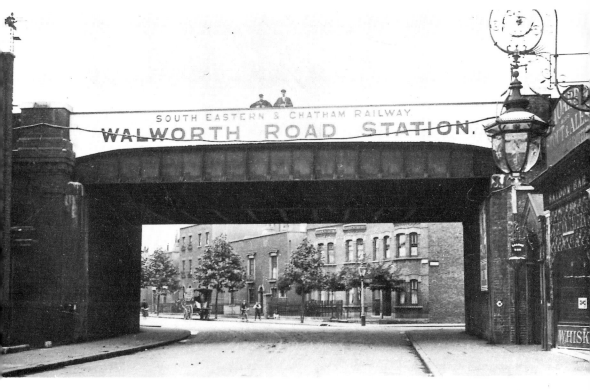

The Vestry Depot is marked on the left page of this 1895 edition and a tram depot is nearby. In later records, the line was listed as the Borough of Southwark Dust Sidings. Near the centre of the right page is Walworth Road station, the road of that name running along the upper border of the map.

62. Opened as Camberwell Gate on 1st May 1863, the elevated station was renamed Walworth Road in January 1865. When the route was quadrupled, only a short down platform was provided on the main line. (Lens of Sutton)

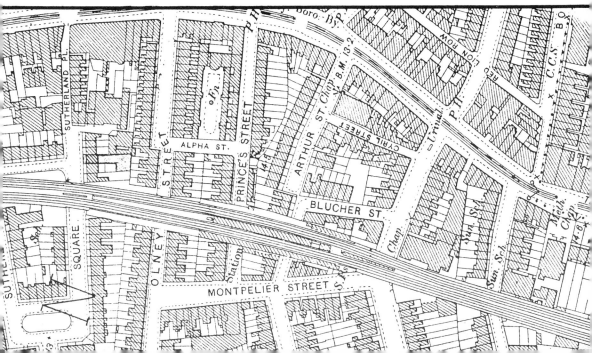

63. A train to West Croydon passes the stairwell of the former island platform, while passing over Ruskin Street. The station closed on 3rd April 1916, when the services to Moorgate ceased. The rake of three wooden coaches has been augmented by a wide steel one. (South London Press)

64. Walworth Road signal box closed on 31st December 1962. This southward view includes levers for operating the detonator placing machine, visible between the tracks. (South London Press)

CAMBERWELL

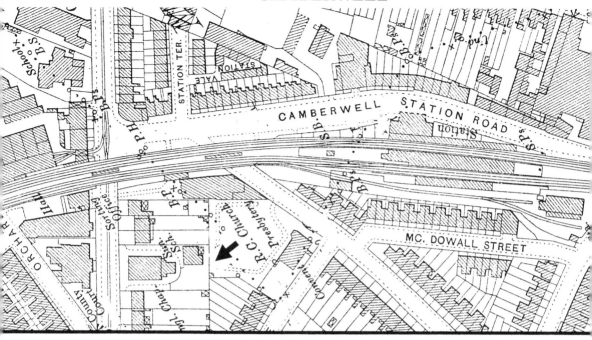

Opened on 6th October 1862, the suffix "New Road" was in use between 1863 and 1908. Camberwell New Road is shown with a single track tramway, which has a depot adjacent to the railway. This map is dated 1895. Almost a century later, the public house (PH) was still named "The Station".

65. Passenger services were withdrawn on 3rd April 1916 but goods facilities remained until 18th April 1964. Out of view, a C class 0-6-0 had hauled the train out of Herne Hill sidings and was now banking it over the crossover and round the steep curve at Loughborough Junction. C class no.31576 is the train engine on 28th February 1957. The 25 lever signal box closed on 15th February 1970. In 1990 there was an active campaign to have the station reopened. (R.C.Riley)

LOUGHBOROUGH JUNCTION

66. The elevated railway system of the district dominated many streets but generated much business accommodation in the arches. This picture is from a 19th century postcard Loughborough Park was developed for housing in 1844. (Lens of Sutton)

67. The first platforms were on the Brixton line (foreground) and were in use between October 1864 and April 1916. Until December 1872, they were named Brixton Junction, and no trace remained when photographed in 1954. On July 1st 1872, three platforms (see map) were provided on the Herne Hill lines, together with two on the Denmark Hill route (left), and were known as Loughborough Road until 1st December 1872. (R.C.Riley)

68. The platforms on the Denmark Hill curve (background) were closed on 12th July 1925, as was the down through platform to Herne Hill (centre). Subsequently, the down lines were reduced from two to one and the island platform was widened. (Lens of Sutton)

KING'S COLLEGE HOSPITAL

SOUTH EASTERN & CHATHAM RAILWAY

L.B. & S.C.R. SOUTH LONDON LINE

VAUGHAN ROAD

BREDON ROAD

CONDERTON ROAD

BENGEWORTH ROAD

Cambria Junction

NORTHWAY ROAD

CAMBRIA ROAD

The 1916 survey has the lines from Holborn Viaduct at the top; those to Victoria lower left; to Herne Hill lower centre, with Cambria Junction and the Denmark Hill route on the right. Also on the right is King's College Hospital which moved from Portugal Street (WC2) and now fails to reveal its identity to rail passengers. Nearby are the South London Power Co's sidings.

69. The wide island platform is in the centre and the lines to Denmark Hill are on the left of this 1956 photograph. The signals are for the crossovers on the quadruple track which starts north of the station. (British Rail)

70. A grimy class O1, no.31048, creaks over the crossover at the end of the island platform on a gloomy day in May 1959. The signal box is partially obscured by steam. (P.Hay)

71. The lofty signal box was known as "The Tower" and was once one of the busiest on the LCDR system. It had 54 levers and closed on 29th November 1981, since when the area has been controlled from the Victoria Panel, situated at Clapham Junction. (J.Scrace)

S. E. & C. & MET. RYS. (SEE BACK
Available Day of issue ONLY
LOUGHBORO' JUNCTION to
LOUGHBORO' JUNC   LOUGHBORO' JUNC
ALDERSGATE ST.
VIA SNOW HILL
4d Third Class 4d
ALDERSGATE ST   ALDERSGATE ST
8183   8183

72. In 1990, access was through the arch adjacent to Coldharbour Lane and the ticket office had been moved to the top of the steps (centre, in shadow). A 30-minute interval service was available to Luton and Guildford. The TV monitor (centre) permits driver-only operation of the class 319 units. (J.Scrace)

CAMBRIA JUNCTION

73. On the left are the quadruple tracks from Victoria which are on a falling gradient from the bridge over the Loughborough Junction - Herne Hill line. The curve from Loughborough Junction is behind no.7660, seen on 11th August 1970. (J.Scrace)

74. Looking in the other direction, on the same day, we see the 12.00 Sevenoaks to Holborn Viaduct service. The lines were laid by the LBSCR but the pair on the left were used by the LCDR. (J.Scrace)

DENMARK HILL

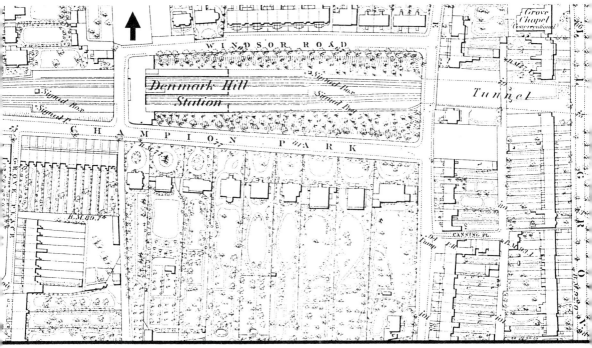

The 1st edition of about 1870 shows the spacious houses, with extensive gardens, that once provided first class passengers to City and West End destinations.

75. The ornate exterior loses some of its impact being in a side turning with no opportunity for distant viewing. The sign to the "Telegraph Office" is a reminder that the LCDR's Metropolitan Extension was largely financed by the sale of its telegraph system.
(Lens of Sutton)

76. To counteract the loss of over a million passengers per annum to the electrified tramways, the LBSCR decided to electrify their South London Line from Victoria to London Bridge. Overhead supply at 6700 volts AC was chosen and services commenced on 1st December 1909. A SECR Holborn Viaduct to Orpington service departs on 11th July 1920. (A.Crawforth/J.R.W.Kirkby coll.)

77. A South London Line train leaves for London Bridge on 7th March 1953, revealing the low roof line at the end of the rear coach, which once carried the pantograph. Overhead collection ended on 17th June 1928 and the signal box ceased to control the former LCDR lines on 8th March 1959. (R.C.Riley)

78. A 1967 eastward view shows that, by then, colour light signalling had been introduced on both Eastern and Central Division lines. This part of the route required heavy civil engineering work and extensive brickwork in the mid-1860s. (British Rail)

79. Although transfer freight via Farringdon ceased in 1969, this part of the route continues to carry a considerable freight traffic, some running via the West London Line. No.E6004 runs west with oil tanks on 11th August 1970. (J.Scrace)

80. On the same day, unit no.5034 emerges from the 132yd long Grove Tunnel, over which run Grove Lane and Camberwell Grove. The train is the 13.00 Sevenoaks to Holborn Viaduct service. (J.Scrace)

81. Since May 1988, Sevenoaks services have been worked by class 319 units, this one having originated at Cricklewood at 11.41 on 31st March 1989. In the distance, the line dips through the 63yd Denmark Hill Tunnel. (A.Dasi-Sutton)

82. On the same day, no.56014 roared through with empty coal hoppers from Northfleet, bound for Toton. Cement and aggregates are other important bulk commodities regularly passing along the route.. (A.Dasi-Sutton)

83. A Kent coast service speeds under the buildings which were severely damaged by fire in 1980. Pressure from the Camberwell Society prevented their demolition and resulted in the small part on the right being renovated as a booking hall and office, while the remainder is used as licensed premises, decorated with railway memorabilia. A Civic Trust Award was received. The restored traditional lighting was photographed on 9th November 1989. (A.C.Mott)

PECKHAM RYE

84. These are the northern platforms provided for the LCDR, the LBSCR platforms being on the right. The palatial booking hall between them is still in use. This and the next two photographs were taken on 7th March 1953. (R.C.Riley)

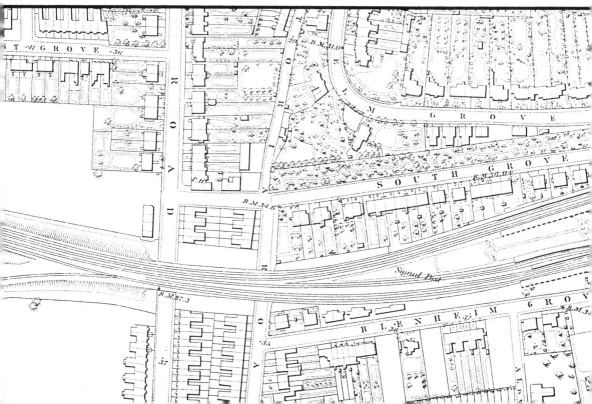

85. The B Box was at the east end of the LCDR down platform while A Box was at the east end of the LBSCR up platform and C was near the junction. About 400 yds east of the station, LCDR trains regained their own tracks, all four lines from Cambria Junction belonging to the LBSCR. This box closed on 8th March 1959. (R.C.Riley)

The 1st edition from about 1868 has the LCDR lines from Denmark Hill to Nunhead running from top left to lower right. The LBSCR Tulse Hill to London Bridge lines go from lower left to top right. Their carriage sheds were erected later, in the fork of the lines on the left.

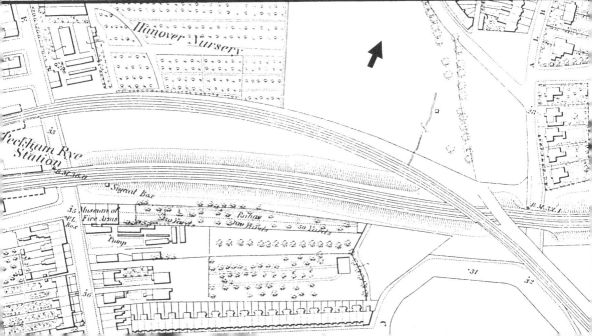

86. In the space between the two routes east of the station, the LNWR and the MR jointly established a coal depot in 1891. Instead of employing gravity as at the earlier depots, a hoist was installed in the black tower, which linked with low level sidings (right). In 1945, three men handled 15,000 tons but traffic ceased in 1958. (R.C.Riley)

87. In 1960, the station was extensively reconstructed and the former LBSCR side received an island platform. This is the westward view from the main building on 27th October. (British Rail)

88. It is now difficult to appreciate the imposing architecture from Rye Lane. The rebuilt canopies can be seen as nos.33020 and 33060 run through from Nunhead on 12th February 1990. (J.Scrace)

89. On the same day, empty stock passes the site of the former coal depot, having crossed Cow Lane bridge over the London Bridge lines. This was boundary point between the LCDR and LBSCR property. The bridge was destroyed by the blast from a flying bomb (doodlebug) on 13th July 1944. Within ten days a trestle bridge was in use! (J.Scrace)

NUNHEAD

90. The centre road was for use by up trains to London or terminating branch trains. It appears that the up island platform (left) had received a canopy extension at some time, no doubt due to complaints by the public. This photograph was taken in 1921, four years before the station was demolished. (P.Rutherford)

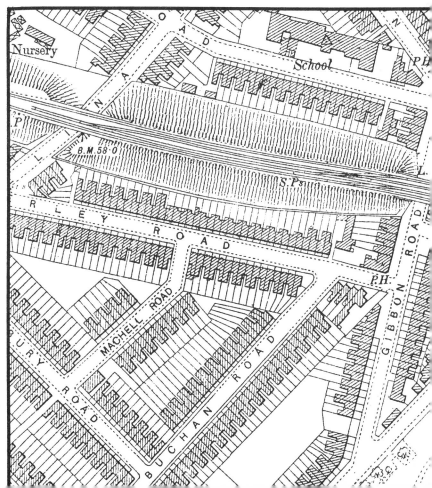

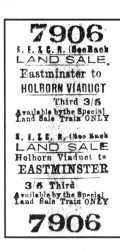

When opened on 1st August 1865, the line between Peckham Rye and Crystal Palace had no intermediate stations. Nunhead was opened on 1st September 1871, when the first part of the Greenwich Park branch (right) came into use. This 1897 map has the 1892 Catford Loop line to the right of the Crystal Palace branch at the lower border.

91. A new station, on the other side of Gibbon Road, was opened on 3rd May 1925. It had a wide island platform and a separate booking office, the pointed roof of which is visible on the left. The C class 0-6-0 is probably bound for Hither Green. Until closure in 1952, the Crystal Palace branch diverged in the foreground. (Greenwich Public Library)

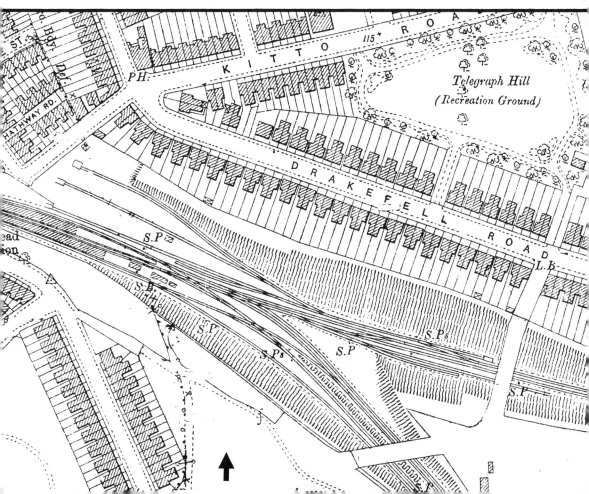

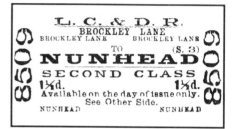

92. A 1952 photograph includes the name of a railway that had not existed for over 50 years and the name of a station that had never officially existed. (J.H.Aston)

93. The down starting signals in May 1953 were for Lewisham (left), Catford Loop (Centre) and Crystal Palace (right). The coal yard had a trailing connection to the down Lewisham line. (J.H.Aston)

94. The signal box had 38 levers in use and was on the south side of the junction, picture no. 91 having been taken from it. It ceased to function on 17th January 1982, having been built in 1925. (J.Scrace)

95. A westward view in February 1990 shows that the up side was fitted with a signal for starting trains in the down direction. (J.Scrace)

96. Use of the 1925 street level booking hall was discontinued in 1990, when a small ticket office was established on the island platform. (J.Scrace)

THE GREENWICH PARK BRANCH

This line was built as part of the continuing war between the LCDR and the SER, in an attempt to take away some of the trade from the latter's London and Greenwich line. It was hoped to continue beyond Greenwich to Woolwich Dockyard by a tunnel under Greenwich Park. The line was not very successful as the journey to Blackfriars and Holborn Viaduct took longer than the SER line to London Bridge, though it did end up on the right side of the Thames for the City. In addition, in the early part of this century trams took away much of the traffic. Every station was adjacent to a tram route. Under the circumstances the SECR must have been quite glad of the opportunity to close the line as a wartime measure in 1917 and never reopen it again. The line was 2¼ miles long from Nunhead to Crooms Hill, Greenwich, and authorised by Act of Parliament on 28th July 1863. It was opened on 18th September 1871 as far as Blackheath Hill. By then, the LCDR had run out of money and the line to Greenwich Park was not opened until seventeen years later, on 1st October 1888.

97. No.33211 takes the Lewisham line from Nunhead on 14th May 1982, the Catford Loop disappearing behind the sub-station. The signal box and station canopy are visible in the distance, while in the foreground we can see the siding that once led to the four-road goods yard, closed on 2nd April 1962. (J.Petley)

98. The previous picture was taken from the footbridge, a short while before Stratford-based no.37090 appeared with a load of scrap steel from Temple Mills, bound for the steelworks at Sheerness. The footbridge was erected after Aspinall Road bridge collapsed. (J.Petley)

BROCKLEY LANE

99. The station opened in June 1872, nine months after the nearby LBSCR station. The approaching up passenger train is drawn by Kirtley M2 class 4-4-0, its SECR number being 642. The signal is interesting, having up and down arms on the same post. (Lens of Sutton)

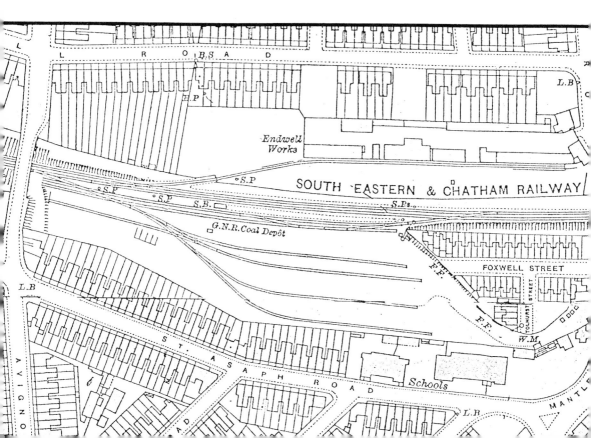

100. The derelict remains of Brockley Lane slumber in August 1928, before the line was refurbished for the Lewisham connection. It shows that the platforms and all the buildings were of wood except the brick built station-master's office (left). St. Peter's Church has lost its pinnacles since the previous photograph, an event which occurred following a storm. (Lens of Sutton)

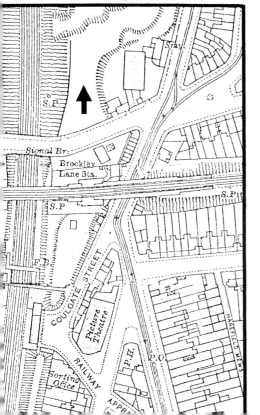

This is the 1916 survey, with the LBSCR's London Bridge - East Croydon line running from north to south. The upside of the yard was opened about twelve years after the first part of the Greenwich line was completed. It was a GNR coal depot and held 40 wagons. GNR coal trains reached it via Farringdon (Street) and Loughborough Junction. It is said that the GNR was allowed to open the yard by the LCDR because the former had subscribed to the latter's Metropolitan Extension from Ludgate Hill to Farringdon Street. The lines on the down side were opened in 1885 and were known as Martins sidings. They were leased to the LNWR and later sublet to Charrington, Warrens Ltd. There was accommodation for 36 wagons. Later Martins sidings served the United Dairies Depot on Endwell Road and the firm of George Robinson and Son Ltd. The entrance to the GNR depot was from Mantle Road and coal wagons turning left had a stiff climb up under the railway bridge. An extra horse was attached to help up the hill. The sidings were closed on 4th May 1970.

101. The station slowly rotted away, as witnessed in August 1928. The branch continued to be used for freight to the nearby depot but to the east of that it was only used for coach berthing between the peak hours.
(Lens of Sutton)

L. C. & D. R.
LOUGHBORO' JUNCTION
LOUGHBORO' JUN   LOUGHBORO' JUN
·TO·   (S. 48)
PECKHAM RYE
THIRD   CLASS
1½d.   1½d.
Available on the day of issue only.
See Other Side.
PECKHAM RYE.   PECKHAM RYE

8336   8336

102. The goods yard closed on 4th May 1970, having been transferred from the Eastern to the Southern Region in 1949. The signal box closed on 7th March 1973 and is seen in April 1976. Soon after closure, the station buildings were used by local boy scouts but now the site has been developed for industrial purposes.
(J.Scrace)

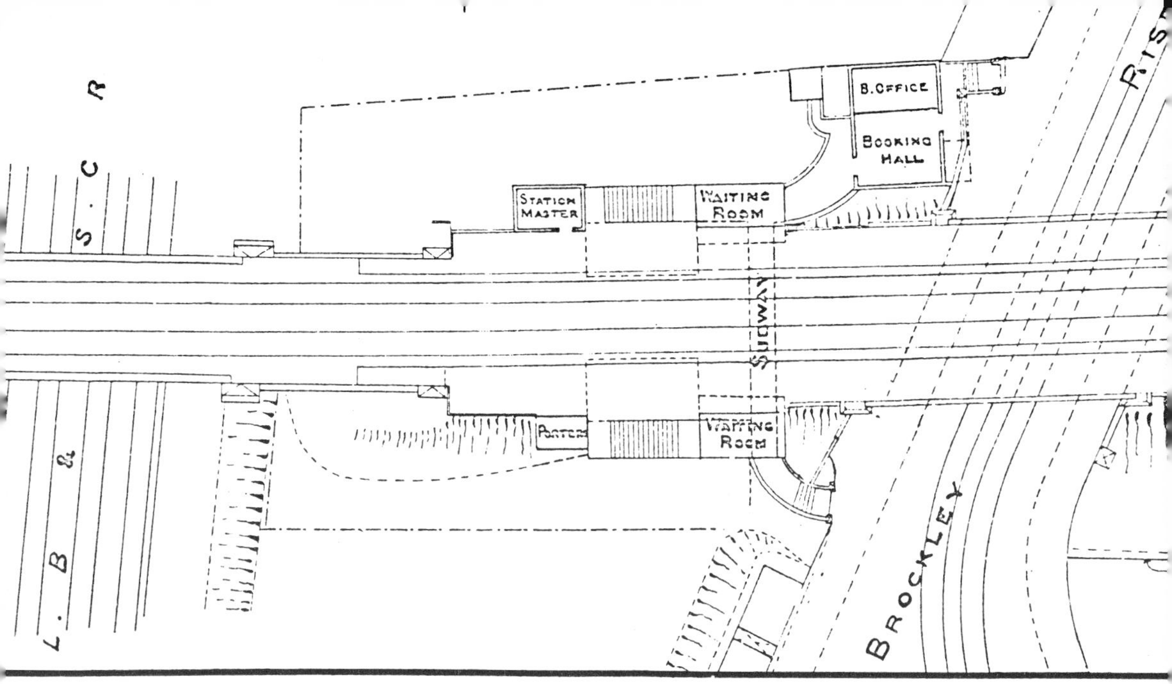

B. OFFICE
BOOKING HALL
STATION MASTER
WAITING ROOM
SUBWAY
PORTERS
WAITING ROOM
BROCKLEY
L. B. & S. C R

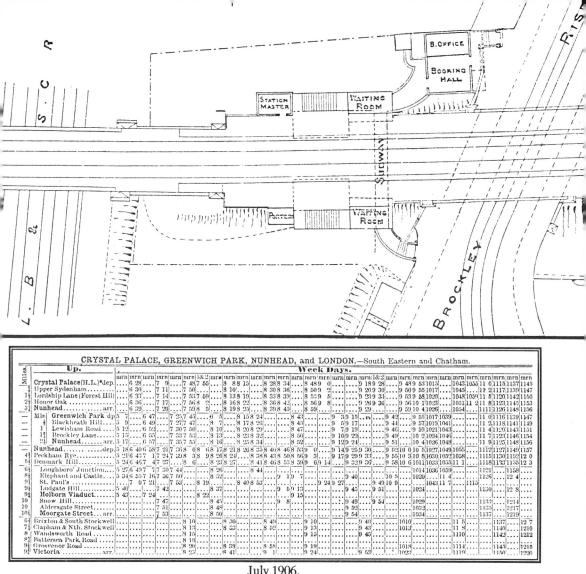

CRYSTAL PALACE, GREENWICH PARK, NUNHEAD, and LONDON.—South Eastern and Chatham.

Miles.	Up.	Week Days.																													
		mrn	mrn	mrn	mrn	mrn	mrn	1&2	mrn	mrn	mrn	mrn	mrn	mrn	mrn	mrn	mrn	mrn	mrn	mrn	1&2	mrn	mrn	mrn	mrn	mrn	mrn	mrn	mrn	mrn	mrn	mrn
	Crystal Palace (H.L.)*dep.	....	6 28	....	7 9	....	7 48	7 55	....	8 8	8 15	....	8 28	8 34	....	8 48	9 0	....	....	9 18	9 28	....	9 48	9 53	1015	....	1043	1055	11 0	1115	1137	1145
¾	Upper Sydenham	....	6 30	....	7 11	....	7 50	....	....	8 10	....	....	8 30	8 36	....	8 50	9 2	....	....	9 20	9 30	....	9 50	9 55	1017	....	1045	....	11 2	1117	1139	1147
1½	Lordship Lane (Forest Hill)	....	6 33	....	7 14	....	7 53	7 59	....	8 13	8 19	....	8 33	8 39	....	8 53	9 5	....	....	9 23	9 33	....	9 53	9 58	1020	....	1048	1059	11 5	1120	1142	1150
2¼	Honor Oak	....	6 36	....	7 17	....	7 56	8 2	....	8 16	8 22	....	8 36	8 42	....	8 56	9 8	....	....	9 26	9 36	....	9 56	10 1	1023	....	1051	11 2	11 8	1123	1145	1153
3¼	Nunhead arr.	....	6 39	....	7 20	....	7 59	8 5	....	8 19	8 25	....	8 39	8 45	....	8 59	....	....	....	9 29	....	....	9 59	10 4	1026	....	1054	....	1111	1126	1148	1156
—	Mls Greenwich Park dp	5 7	....	6 47	....	7 25	7 45	....	8 5	....	8 15	8 24	....	....	8 43	....	....	9 3	9 15	....	....	9 42	....	9 55	1017	1039	....	....	11 0	1116	1139	1147
—	½ Blackheath Hill	5 9	....	6 49	....	7 27	7 47	....	8 7	....	8 17	8 26	....	....	8 45	....	....	9 5	9 17	....	....	9 44	....	9 57	1019	1041	....	....	11 2	1118	1141	1149
—	1 Lewisham Road	5 12	....	6 52	....	7 30	7 50	....	8 10	....	8 20	8 29	....	....	8 47	....	....	9 7	9 19	....	....	9 46	....	9 59	1021	1043	....	....	11 4	1120	1143	1151
—	1¾ Brockley Lane	5 15	....	6 55	....	7 33	7 53	....	8 13	....	8 23	8 32	....	....	8 50	....	....	9 10	9 22	....	....	9 49	....	10 2	1024	1046	....	....	11 7	1123	1146	1154
—	2¼ Nunhead arr.	5 17	....	6 57	....	7 35	7 55	....	8 16	....	8 25	8 34	....	....	8 52	....	....	9 12	9 24	....	....	9 51	....	10 4	1026	1048	....	....	11 9	1125	1148	1156
—	Nunhead dep.	5 18	6 40	6 58	7 21	7 36	8 0	8 6	8 17	8 21	8 26	8 35	8 40	8 46	8 53	9 0	....	9 14	9 25	9 30	....	9 52	10 0	10 5	1027	1049	1055	....	1112	1127	1149	1157
4¾	Peckham Rye	5 21	6 43	7 1	7 24	7 39	8 3	8 9	8 20	8 24	....	8 38	8 43	8 50	8 56	9 3	....	9 17	9 29	9 33	....	9 55	10 3	10 8	1030	1052	1058	....	1115	1130	1152	12 0
5¼	Denmark Hill	5 24	6 46	7 4	7 27	....	8 6	....	8 23	8 27	....	8 41	8 46	8 53	8 59	9 6	9 14	....	9 32	9 36	....	9 58	10 6	1011	1033	1055	11 1	....	1118	1133	1155	12 3
6¼	Loughboro' Junction	5 27	6 49	7 7	7 30	7 44	....	....	8 26	....	....	8 44	....	....	....	....	....	....	....	....	....	....	....	1014	1036	1059	....	....	1121	....	1158	....
8¼	Elephant and Castle	5 34	6 55	7 16	7 36	7 50	....	....	8 32	....	....	....	....	9 1	9 7	....	....	....	9 40	....	....	10 5	....	1020	....	11 4	....	....	1126	....	12 4	....
9¼	St. Paul's	....	7 0	7 21	....	7 53	....	8 19	....	....	8 40	8 53	....	....	....	....	9 24	9 27	....	....	9 49	10 9	....	....	1043	11 7	....	1115	....	....	....	....
9¼	Ludgate Hill	5 40	....	....	7 42	....	....	....	8 37	....	....	....	....	9 5	9 13	....	....	....	9 45	....	9 51	....	....	1024	....	....	....	....	1130	....	12 8	....
9¼	Holborn Viaduct	5 43	....	7 24	....	....	....	8 22	....	....	....	....	....	....	9 15	....	....	....	....	....	....	....	....	....	....	....	....	....	....	....	....	....
10	Snow Hill	....	....	....	7 47	....	....	....	8 45	....	....	....	....	9 8	....	....	....	....	9 49	....	9 54	....	....	1029	....	....	....	....	1133	....	1214	....
10	Aldersgate Street	....	....	....	7 51	....	....	....	8 48	....	....	....	....	....	....	....	....	....	9 52	....	....	....	....	1032	....	....	....	....	1135	....	1217	....
10¼	Moorgate Street arr.	....	....	....	7 53	....	....	....	8 50	....	....	....	....	....	....	....	....	....	9 54	....	....	....	....	1034	....	....	....	....	1137	....	1219	....
6¾	Brixton & South Stockwell	....	....	....	....	....	8 10	....	....	8 30	....	....	8 49	....	....	9 10	....	....	....	9 40	....	....	1010	....	....	....	11 5	....	....	1137	....	12 7
7¾	Clapham & Nth. Stockwell	....	....	....	....	....	8 13	....	....	8 33	....	....	8 52	....	....	9 13	....	....	....	9 43	....	....	1013	....	....	....	11 8	....	....	1140	....	1210
8	Wandsworth Road	....	....	....	....	....	8 15	....	....	....	....	....	....	....	....	9 15	....	....	....	9 45	....	....	....	....	....	....	1110	....	....	1142	....	1212
8¾	Battersea Park Road	....	....	....	....	....	8 18	....	....	....	....	....	....	....	....	....	....	....	....	....	....	....	....	....	....	....	....	....	....	....	....	....
9¼	Grosvenor Road	....	....	....	....	....	8 20	....	....	8 38	....	....	8 58	....	....	9 19	....	....	....	....	....	....	1018	....	....	....	1114	....	....	1145	....	1215
9¾	Victoria arr.	....	....	....	....	....	8 25	....	....	8 41	....	....	9 1	....	....	9 24	....	....	....	9 53	....	....	1023	....	....	....	1119	....	....	1150	....	1220

July 1906.

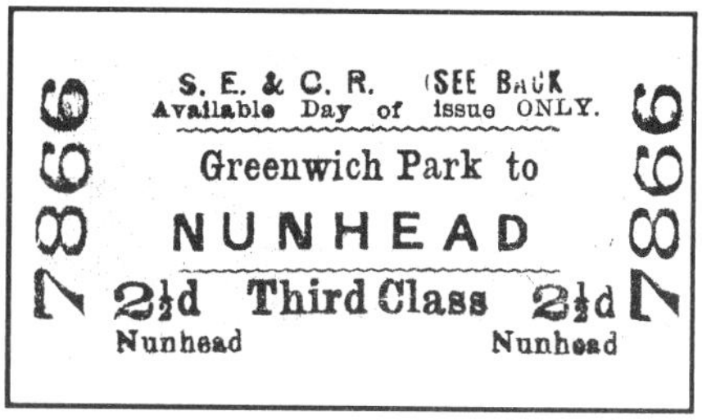

S. E. & C. R. (SEE BACK
Available Day of issue ONLY.
Greenwich Park to
NUNHEAD
7866
2½d Third Class 2½d
Nunhead Nunhead
7866

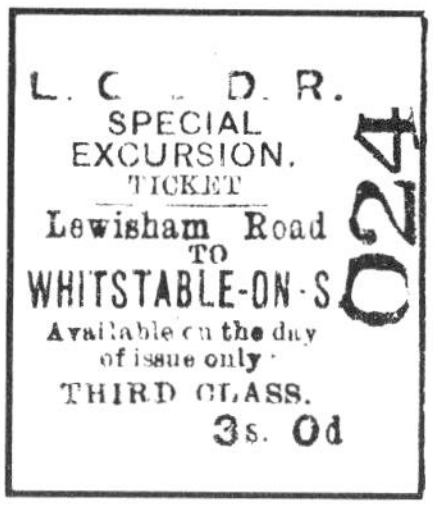

L. C. D. R.
SPECIAL
EXCURSION.
TICKET
Lewisham Road
TO
WHITSTABLE-ON-S
Available on the day
of issue only
THIRD CLASS.
3s. 0d
024

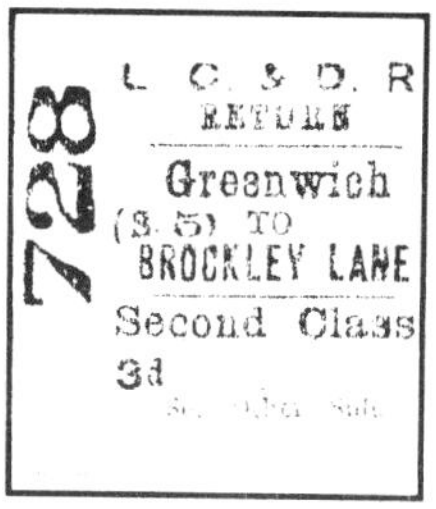

728
L. C. & D. R
RETURN
Greenwich
(S. 5) TO
BROCKLEY LANE
Second Class
3d

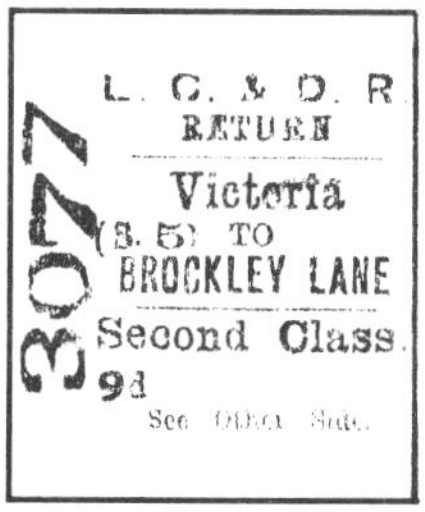

3077
L. C. & D. R
RETURN
Victoria
(S. 5) TO
BROCKLEY LANE
Second Class
9d
See Other Side

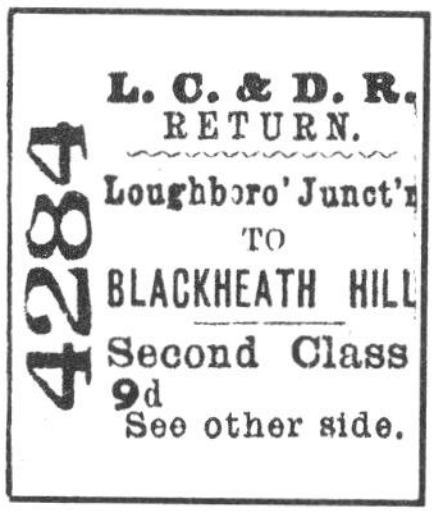

4284
L. C. & D. R.
RETURN.
Loughboro' Junct'n
TO
BLACKHEATH HILL
Second Class
9d
See other side.

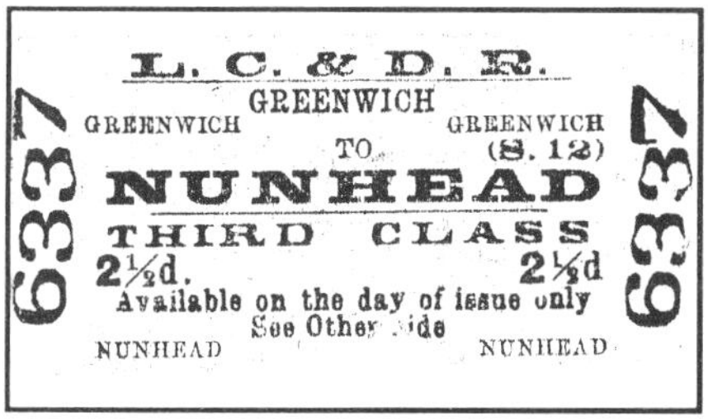

6337
L. C. & D. R.
GREENWICH
GREENWICH TO GREENWICH
(S. 12)
NUNHEAD
THIRD CLASS
2½d. 2½d
Available on the day of issue only
See Other Side
NUNHEAD NUNHEAD
6337

LEWISHAM ROAD

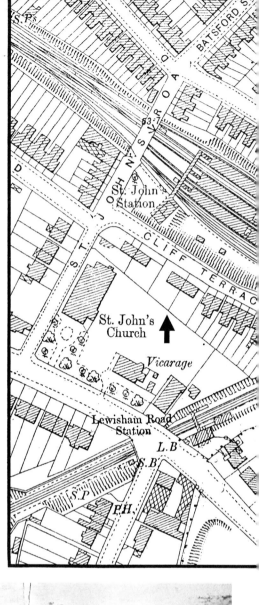

103. The station opened on 18th September 1871, the platforms being seen from the overbridge, looking north towards Greenwich. Passengers who had to wait on the down platform had no shelter at all. The train consists of a seven coach set of four-wheeled LCDR coaches, no longer oil-lit. The bridge beyond the end of the platform spans the SER line, near which stand the magnificent double telegraph poles.
(Lewisham Local History Archives)

The proximity of the SER's St. John's station is evident on this 1897 map. Electric trams commenced running along Lewisham Way in 1906.

←——→

104. The booking office on Lewisham Way (previously Lewisham High Road) stood at the top of Loampit Hill. The picture was taken in about 1918 and shows a wartime potato queue. The coal merchant's office subsequently became a snack bar but has now been demolished. The stationmaster's house is just visible, to the left of the station roof (Lewisham Local History Archives)

←——

105. The track appears to have been deliberately blocked by sleepers and there is a length of narrow gauge track attached to the standard gauge sleepers under the bridge. The cabling at the sides of the line suggests this picture was taken about the time the line was being converted to the Lewisham-Nunhead Loop Line. The series of road bridges crossing the line are successively Lewisham High Road (now Lewisham Way) and Tressilian and Breakspears Roads. (Lens of Sutton)

106. The booking office still stood in August 1989, complete with forecourt and gates. The internal fittings are said to be little changed. At various times it has served as a scout hut, a greengrocers, an antique shop and now deals in wood and wood products. (P.R.Davis)

107. Traces of the line remained for long after closure and partial demolition. This trackless bridge over Brookmill Road, between Lewisham Road and Blackheath Hill, was photographed in 1969 but was later demolished. Brookmill Park is visible on the right beyond the bridge.
(Lewisham Local History Archives)

The 1916 survey shows the densely developed area through which construction was so expensive. Blackheath Hill station is left of centre. During the period when stock was stored on the branch near Nunhead, it is reputed that an insecurely braked set ran down into Blackheath Hill Tunnel and its whereabouts was unknown for two weeks.

BLACKHEATH HILL

108. This was the terminus of the branch from 18th September 1871 until 1st October 1888. An eastward view shows the construction to have been of timber and that a shelter was provided on the up platform. (Lens of Sutton)

109. Eastwards, the line passed under Lewisham Road and over the Ravensbourne River. The scene was recorded in 1928, by which time the outer rails were obscured by grass. (Lens of Sutton)

GREENWICH PARK

110. When finally completed this must have been a quite impressive branch line terminus with its three platforms, engine release road, engine pit and siding behind the signal box for a spare engine. There was a water crane on the island platform. An oil lit train waits to depart behind 0-4-2T no.89 *Mona*. (Lens of Sutton)

The 1895 edition shows that the terminus was aligned to enable easy connection to be made to the SECR, whose line to Woolwich runs diagonally across the map. After the formation of the SER, the suffix "Park" was added to the name of the terminus, on 1st July 1900. The station master's house is marked in black.

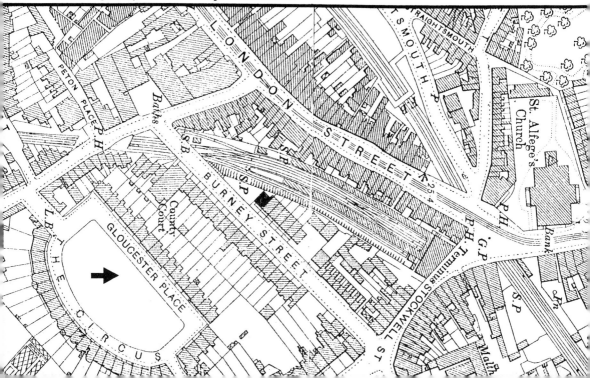

111. Two of these units were formed in 1912 by the SECR for work on this line. They comprised a Wainwright class P 0-6-0T locomotive and two coaches of LCDR origin built in 1897. One was all third and the other composite. Since the leading coach is numbered 3396 the other may be assumed to be 2713 and the locomotive 325 (built in 1910) forming set no. 271. (Lens of Sutton)

112. The signal box is close to Burney Street bridge and was comprehensively equipped - note the treadles each side of the points of the engine release road. (Lens of Sutton)

113. Greenwich was a popular resort for day visits on public holidays - hence the generous provision of canopies for the inevitable rain on such occasions. Business travel was not the only motive for constructing the branch. (Lens of Sutton)

114. For some years the station was in use as a billiard hall. Before demolition in the 1960s, it was used by a firm of builders. The booking hall had a refreshment room, and first and second class ladies rooms leading off it. Stairs led down to the concourse at the head of the platforms. (Lens of Sutton)

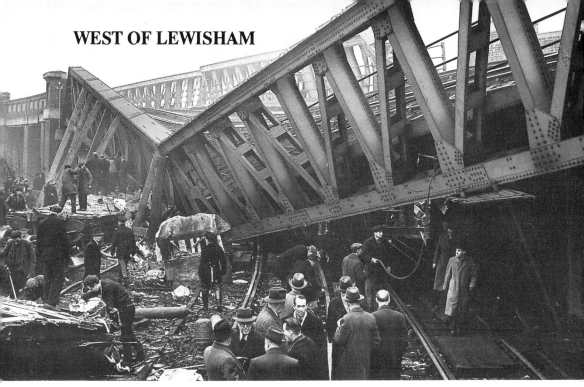

115.   The bridge carrying the Nunhead line over the main line collapsed on 4th December 1957, following a collision under it when the 4.56pm Cannon Street to Ramsgate ran into the rear of the 5.18pm Charing Cross to Hayes, in dense fog. About to run over the bridge was the 5.22pm Holborn Viaduct to Dartford, which stopped with the leading coach at an alarming angle but not derailed. This is commonly known as the St. Johns accident. (British Rail)

116.   The 300 tons of steelwork was cut up and a trestle bridge was brought into use on 13th January 1958. Passing under it on 30th August 1958 is the 11.02 Ramsgate to Charing Cross service, headed by no. 34021 *Dartmoor*. Lewisham station is in the left background. (J.Scrace)

LEWISHAM

The 1895 survey marks the then simple
layout, with the 1891 tram tracks shown in
Lewisham Road.

117. Lewisham first became a junction when
the SER's line to Chislehurst opened on 1st
July 1865. Previously the station was just an
intermediate one on the London Bridge to
Woolwich line, opened on 30th July 1849. A
train takes the Blackheath route in this un-
dated view.   (Lens of Sutton)

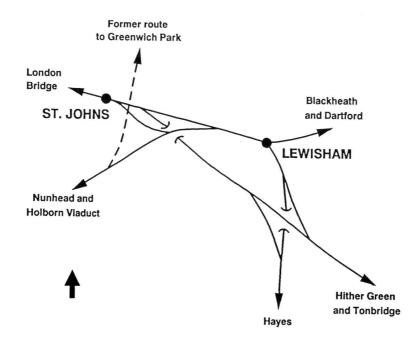

Former route
to Greenwich Park

London
Bridge

ST. JOHNS

Blackheath
and Dartford

LEWISHAM

Nunhead and
Holborn Viaduct

Hither Green
and Tonbridge

Hayes

118. The formation of the SR in 1923 resulted in major rearrangements of junctions in a number of locations. Here, connections were added from Lewisham to the former Greenwich Park branch, near Lewisham Road station. They were primarily intended to take cross-London transfer freight trains that previously ran via London Bridge, and are seen rising on the left. (C.R.L.Coles)

119. Nos. 31786 and 31749 take a LCGB Railtour from the Nunhead to the Blackheath lines on 11th June 1961. The itinerary included Strood, Hawkhurst, Tonbridge and Tenterden, returning to London via Sevenoaks and Ladywell. (J.Scrace)

S. E. & C. R. See Back
Available Day of issue ONLY.

NUNHEAD JUNC. to

LEWISHAM ROAD

3d   First   3d

LEWISHAM ROAD   LEWISHAM ROAD

5600   5600

120. The Nunhead-Lewisham connection (centre background) was electrified on 16th July 1933 and began to carry peak hour trains between Blackfriars and the Dartford lines from 30th September 1935. Apart from suspension during WWII, the route has done so ever since. (Lens of Sutton)

121. The 10.22 Southampton to Halling tankers were hauled by no.33027 on 22nd July 1986. In addition to seeing a variety of freight services, Lewisham has an excellent passenger service to London Bridge and beyond, but only peak hour trains to Blackfriars. (J.Scrace)

SOUTHERN RAILWAY.
Restall's Half-Day Excursion.
Available as advertised.

Nunhead to

Nunhead   Nunhead
Broadstairs, Dumpton Pk.   Broadstairs, Dumpton Pk.
Margate or Ramsgate   Margate or Ramsgate

BROADSTAIRS, DUMPTON PARK,
MARGATE or RAMSGATE and BACK

THIRD CLASS   THIRD CLASS
FOR CONDITIONS SEE BACK.

0491   0491

MP Middleton Press

Easebourne Lane, Midhurst. West Sussex. GU29 9AZ
(0730) 813169

BRANCH LINES

BRANCH LINES TO MIDHURST
BRANCH LINES AROUND MIDHURST
BRANCH LINES TO HORSHAM
BRANCH LINES TO EAST GRINSTEAD
BRANCH LINES TO ALTON
BRANCH LINE TO HAYLING
BRANCH LINE TO SOUTHWOLD
BRANCH LINE TO TENTERDEN
BRANCH LINES TO NEWPORT
BRANCH LINES TO TUNBRIDGE WELLS
BRANCH LINE TO SWANAGE
BRANCH LINES TO LONGMOOR
BRANCH LINE TO LYME REGIS
BRANCH LINE TO FAIRFORD
BRANCH LINE TO ALLHALLOWS
BRANCH LINES AROUND ASCOT
BRANCH LINES AROUND WEYMOUTH
BRANCH LINE TO HAWKHURST
BRANCH LINES AROUND EFFINGHAM JNC
BRANCH LINE TO MINEHEAD

SOUTH COAST RAILWAYS

CHICHESTER TO PORTSMOUTH
BRIGHTON TO EASTBOURNE
RYDE TO VENTNOR
EASTBOURNE TO HASTINGS
PORTSMOUTH TO SOUTHAMPTON
HASTINGS TO ASHFORD
SOUTHAMPTON TO BOURNEMOUTH
ASHFORD TO DOVER
BOURNEMOUTH TO WEYMOUTH
DOVER TO RAMSGATE

SOUTHERN MAIN LINES

HAYWARDS HEATH TO SEAFORD
EPSOM TO HORSHAM
CRAWLEY TO LITTLEHAMPTON
THREE BRIDGES TO BRIGHTON
WATERLOO TO WOKING
VICTORIA TO EAST CROYDON
TONBRIDGE TO HASTINGS
EAST CROYDON TO THREE BRIDGES
WOKING TO SOUTHAMPTON
WATERLOO TO WINDSOR
LONDON BRIDGE TO EAST CROYDON

COUNTRY RAILWAY ROUTES

BOURNEMOUTH TO EVERCREECH JNC
READING TO GUILDFORD
WOKING TO ALTON
BATH TO EVERCREECH JUNCTION
GUILDFORD TO REDHILL
EAST KENT LIGHT RAILWAY
FAREHAM TO SALISBURY
BURNHAM TO EVERCREECH JUNCTION
REDHILL TO ASHFORD
YEOVIL TO DORCHESTER
ANDOVER TO SOUTHAMPTON

LONDON SUBURBAN RAILWAYS

CHARING CROSS TO DARTFORD
HOLBORN VIADUCT TO LEWISHAM

STEAMING THROUGH

STEAMING THROUGH EAST HANTS
STEAMING THROUGH SURREY
STEAMING THROUGH WEST SUSSEX
STEAMING THROUGH THE ISLE OF WIGHT
STEAMING THROUGH WEST HANTS

OTHER RAILWAY BOOKS

GARRAWAY FATHER & SON
LONDON CHATHAM & DOVER RAILWAY
INDUSTRIAL RAILWAYS OF THE S. EAST
WEST SUSSEX RAILWAYS IN THE 1980s
SOUTH EASTERN RAILWAY - due late 1990

OTHER BOOKS

MIDHURST TOWN THEN & NOW
EAST GRINSTEAD THEN & NOW

WALKS IN THE WESTERN HIGH WEALD
TILLINGBOURNE BUS STORY

MILITARY DEFENCE OF WEST SUSSEX
BATTLE OVER SUSSEX 1940

SURREY WATERWAYS
KENT AND EAST SUSSEX WATERWAYS